NEW Baja

Handbook for the Off-Pavement Motorist in Lower California

James T. Crow

BOND/PARKHURST BOOKS

By the same author:
Four Wheel Drive Handbook
(with Cameron A. Warren)
American Road Race of Champions, 1970
Survival of a Species: The Elephant Seal

ISBN 0-87880-020-4

Library of Congress Card No. 73-81325

BOND/PARKHURST PUBLICATIONS, NEWPORT BEACH, CALIFORNIA

PRINTED IN THE UNITED STATES OF AMERICA

Contents

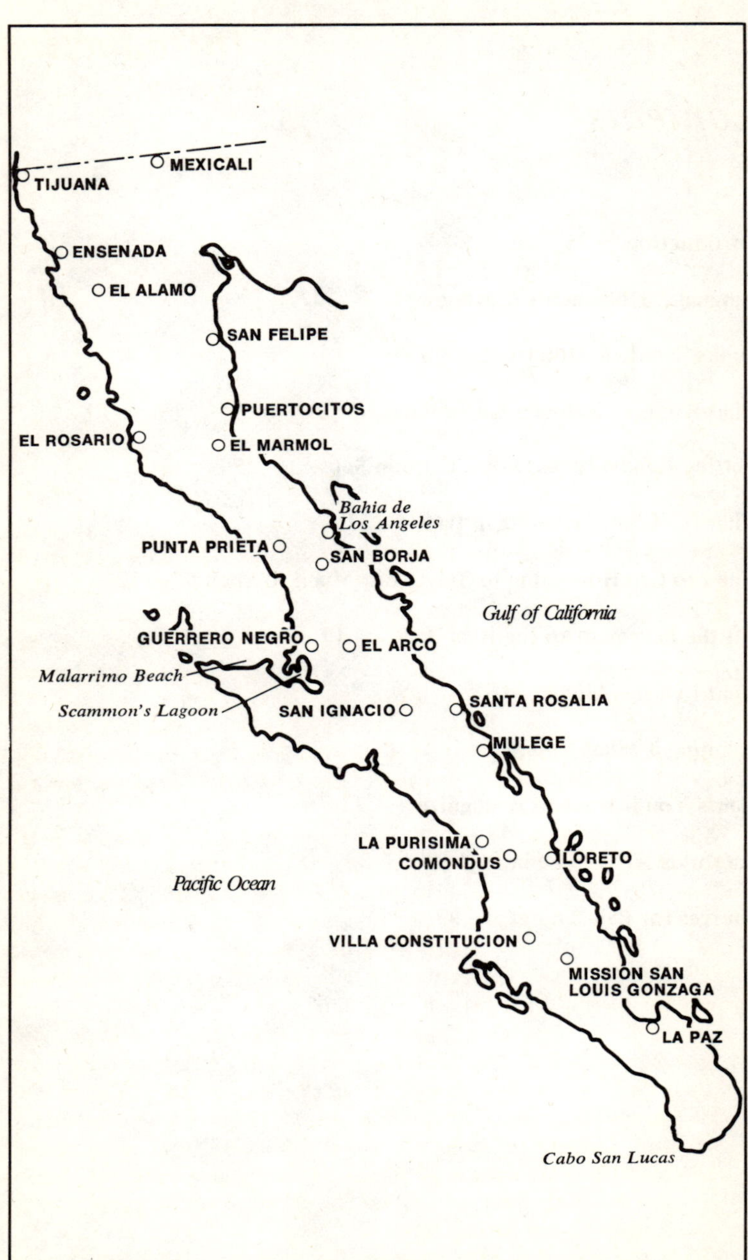

MEXICALI
TIJUANA
ENSENADA
EL ALAMO
SAN FELIPE
PUERTOCITOS
EL ROSARIO
EL MARMOL
Bahia de Los Angeles
PUNTA PRIETA
SAN BORJA
Gulf of California
GUERRERO NEGRO
EL ARCO
Malarrimo Beach
Scammon's Lagoon
SAN IGNACIO
SANTA ROSALIA
MULEGE
LA PURISIMA
COMONDUS
LORETO
Pacific Ocean
VILLA CONSTITUCION
MISSION SAN
LOUIS GONZAGA
LA PAZ
Cabo San Lucas

THIS IS A book about Baja California. It is neither a guidebook, a history book, a geography text, nor a social study. It is, rather, one Baja buff's attempt to open a small door through which others—whether they've never been there at all, or who have been but don't feel they qualify as experts— can see that they too can go and enjoy that barely charted land where the real Baja lies.

It is called the *New Baja Handbook* not only because it is a revised edition of the *Baja Handbook* I wrote in 1970 but also because Baja itself has changed so much that it is a new and different place than the one I wrote about only three years ago.

What makes Baja "new" at this point in its long history is the completion of the paved road running from the northern border all the way to the tip of the peninsula. There have been many changes since a band of mutineers led by Fortun Ximenez sailed into the bay of La Paz in late 1533 or early 1534. But the new highway will wreak more changes in the old peninsula than any other single event since the coming of the white man.

For those of us who consider ourselves old hands in Baja, these changes are viewed with a twinge of sadness. We have, up until now, regarded Baja as our own special province, a place that belonged only to the intrepid traveler of uncommon self-sufficiency who was able to do without motels, or restaurants, or even roads that were clearly marked. We liked Baja the way it was and we regret having it opened up so anyone with four wheels and a deck of credit cards can go motoring through our special land.

That's the way it is with progress, however, and while we're sorry to have Baja be something less than it was, we also have to admit that the new road is going to be good for the economy of the peninsula. We also realize that there's lots of the "old" Baja still there, and the fact that you'll be able to zip from the border to the tip in a couple or three days hasn't destroyed it completely. There's still going to be lots of the "real" Baja left, out-of-the-way places that still call for a certain amount of adventurousness, a certain measure of independence and a little more self-sufficiency than can be expected of the credit-card tourist.

That's really what this book is about, the real Baja that lies beyond the edge of the paved road, and for all my sour grapes there's still enough of that left for all of us. So come to the real Baja and enjoy it!

Language, Documents & Money

BAJA CALIFORNIA, and you'd better believe it, is a foreign country. To the average American, even a trip to Europe is far less "foreign" than a visit to Baja. The language is different, the money is different, the units of measurements are different, the customs are different, the life is different. It's a strange, exotic land like no other place on earth.

The Baja you'll encounter once you get away from the tourist centers and off the pavement would have to be classified as primitive. But primitive doesn't mean retarded or savage. There's little violence in the people of Baja once you get away from the heavily populated border areas and these, I won't lie to you, are ugly and depressing. The real Baja is desert, to be sure, but if the visitor practices nothing more than common sense, he's no doubt safer in Baja than on the streets of his own hometown after dark. The off-pavement parts of Baja are dangerous only in that they are remote. If your vehicle breaks down when you're 50 miles from the main road, by yourself, and nobody knows where you are, you could be in serious trouble. But such hazards are avoidable; it doesn't take any genius to understand that.

THE LANGUAGE

Spanish is the language of Baja California, of course, but it is a somewhat different Spanish than that used in either Spain or mainland Mexico. You can get along with formal Spanish, if you're lucky enough to possess it, but there are many Americanizations that are peculiar to the peninsula. In formal Spanish, for instance, the word for truck is *camion.* But in Baja the natives are far more likely to say *troque* (pronounced "trockay").

But you don't have to speak Spanish Spanish or even Baja Spanish to get along in Baja. It is pleasant to have a few phrases that you can use in salutation but from that point you can make your needs known through the use of a phrase book.

When asking directions in Baja, by the way, it is wise to keep in mind the fact that the Baja resident is a very agreeable, peaceable person and for this reason prefers to tell you what you want to hear. If you ask him if the road ahead is *muy malo* (very bad), he is likely to agree with you. If you had asked *"Es bueno?"* under the same circumstances, he would probably have smiled and agreed to that too. So it's usually better to confine your questions to matters of fact. Like the name of his ranch, or the name of the town. Or where does the road go rather than if this is the right road to so-and-so. If you ask an opinion, he'd rather not be so inhospitable as to disagree with you. Even if the road is terrible and there's a short cut that's miles closer.

BORDER FORMALITIES

Getting across the border into Baja is as easy as anything that can be imagined. You can cross at Tijuana, Tecate or Mexicali and at none of these are there any complicated formalities to be undergone unless you are there on business.

When you go south of the tourist centers near the border (Ensenada on the west coast, San Felipe on the east), you are required to have a *Tarjeta de Turista* (tourist permit). Like some other requirements in Mexico, these are more required in some places than in others. We once spend an hour at Tecate trying to get permits for a trip to Los Angeles Bay only to be told that this document wasn't required unless we were going to mainland Mexico. Admittedly, we've never been asked for our tourist permits except when we were crossing to the mainland but the rules do say you have to have one and it could be troublesome if some official decided to ask for yours and you were summarily classified as an illegal alien because you couldn't produce one.

The tourist permit is available at the border stations at Tecate and Mexicali, and at the checkpoint just south of Maneadero on the other side of Ensenada. They are also available at Mexican National Tourist Offices, Mexican consulates, airline ticket counters and some travel agents in the U.S., but as these must be validated at the *Migracion* office anyway there's little advantage in going through the routine in the States.

To get a tourist permit you need proof of citizenship (passport, birth certificate, armed forces discharge papers, voter's registration receipt, or whatever). There is no charge for this permit and I personally have never found it necessary to give a dollar to the attendant although I understand that some officials do not feel such a gratuity is too much to expect for expediting the preparation of your document.

There's now a new-style permit that is far simpler than the old one since you fill it out yourself rather than wait for it to be typed up by an official. The expected length of your visit is recorded on the permit, so give yourself a few days' grace in case you stay longer than you expect to. You are required to surrender the permit at the border when you leave Mexico and if you can't find anyone to give it to, it is permissible to mail it to the address shown on the permit after you get home.

There is also a multiple-entry permit available at Mexican consulates in case you regularly cross the border. With this you need two (or is it three?) passport-size photographs as well as proof of citizenship.

No health certificate or proof of recent vaccination is required at the present time either for going into Mexico or when returning to the U.S.

If you must take a pet along, and it should be an experienced rough-country traveler before you even consider it, check with the U.S. authorities before going into Mexico. If you have a certificate from a veterinarian attesting that the animal is "clean" and has had a recent rabies shot, there shouldn't be any problem about getting it back across the border. Don't plan on bringing any Mexican animals back, though, unless you are prepared to wait out the quarantine period and go through lots of other red tape.

CAR PERMIT

A car permit is not required in Baja. But one is required for mainland Mexico. So if you're coming down the mainland and taking one of the ferries across to Baja, or if you're going down Baja and then crossing over to the mainland, you do need one. On the mainland you get the car permit at the *aduana* (customs) office just south of the Arizona, New Mexico or Texas border. In Baja you hunt up the *aduana* office in Santa Rosalia or La Paz before you buy your ticket for the ferry.

The procedures for getting a car permit vary from place to place, as such things often do in Mexico. You may be directed to a customs broker who will collect a 2- or 3-dollar fee for filling out the forms, or they may be filled out in the customs office for no charge. When the transaction is complete you will also get a pair of window stickers and if this is applied by still another official, the accepted procedure is to tip him a dollar for his assistance. If you are driving down the mainland, you will be stopped at least once at a check station to make sure all your papers are in order. As you leave mainland Mexico, be sure and surrender the permit at an *aduana* office, otherwise they may suspect that you have sold the car in Mexico, another forbidden practice.

To get a car permit the U.S. registration is required and if you are not the legal owner of the car, you need a notarized statement from the legal owner giving you permission to drive the car in Mexico.

When the form is being filled out you are asked to declare what is in the vehicle; the answer they want is "personal effects," not an itemized list of contents. You will also be asked if you have a radio, or air conditioning, and to declare the number of spare tires and wheels you have with you. If, after declaring such items, you were to arrive at the checkout point without them, it could be troublesome as foreigners are forbidden to sell anything in Mexico unless they have a government permit to do so. Also on the forbidden list in Mexico is for a foreigner to have a 2-way radio in his vehicle. This is not strictly enforced, of course, but if you get questioned about the long antenna on your roof, assure the interrogator that the radio is disconnected.

The car permit is good for one month and that, plus the tourist permit and a valid U.S. drivers license, are the only documents needed by the U.S. traveler in Mexico.

CAR INSURANCE

Unless you have a policy that is specially written to cover travel in Mexico by a company licensed by the Mexican authorities to issue such insurance, you'll need car insurance when you travel in Mexico. The law operates very differently in Mexico, as many Americans have found to their sorrow, and if you are involved in an accident and don't have insurance, it will be inconvenient, to say the least. You could end up waiting in some very unpleasant jail until your case is investigated (which doesn't happen quickly in Mexico), liability assigned (which takes even longer) and settlements agreed upon (you know how lawyers are). So don't take a chance. Buy insurance when you cross the border.

The cost of insurance varies with the value of the vehicle, the coverage you specify and the length of time the policy covers. What you want is "full coverage" and this comes to roughly $1.50 to $2.00 per day, depending on the value you place on the vehicle. When buying insurance, you'll need to show your vehicle registration, that's all. But you should also have a notarized statement from the legal owner of the vehicle giving you permission to take it into Mexico.

Tepeyac and Sanborn are two well known names in the Mexican insurance business. As I've never had to call on them regarding a claim, I don't have any experience in how quickly an adjuster can be expected to arrive, but their offices seem businesslike, which is reassuring anyway. Sanborn also offers a travel log as a part of the package and while this isn't much good for Baja, it is very helpful on the mainland.

MONEY

The monetary unit in Mexico is the peso and at the present time it is worth eight cents in U.S. money—12½ pesos to the dollar—though this may change shortly due to the sinking value of the American buck. U.S. dollars can be exchanged at any bank in Mexico and these will also cash travelers checks. Personally, I find it easier and more convenient to carry U.S. bills of small denomination in Baja. By "small," I mean ones, fives and tens, but mostly ones and fives, as anything larger may completely paralyze the currency flow at a small racho. With a supply of small bills so I can come close to the exact amount, I've never had any trouble spending U.S. money in Baja. Almost invariably the change comes back in pesos and centavos (100 of which makes a peso) and that adds flexibility for the next purchase. Sharpies in the tourist centers may offer to give you a fast count (they are always cheerfully apologetic when they make a mistake) but out in the real Baja I've never encountered anything except scrupulous honesty.

Don't expect to cash a travelers check outside the larger cities and don't bother offering a credit card anyplace except at resorts and hotels that cater to tourists. Diners Club seems to be the most widely accepted credit card, with American Express running a poor third or fourth behind Interbank and Bankmatico.

If all else fails and an emergency has arisen where nothing else is possible, a personal check will often be accepted. This would have to rank as the least popular form of financial settlement, however, as not many of the small independent merchants outside the cities have anything like regular access to a bank.

COMING BACK TO THE U.S.

At the border station coming back, you'll be stopped and questioned by U.S. border officials. There may be a thorough inspection or the guard may do nothing more than ask if you're a U.S. citizen. The line may move right along or you may spend an hour or more waiting in line. If you've been out of the country more than 24 hours, you are permitted to bring back $100 worth of goods duty free. But there are exceptions to this. In California, thanks to the strength of the liquor lobby in Sacramento, a California resident cannot bring any liquor across the California-Mexico border. In other states, and for residents of states other than California, the federal regulations do apply and you can bring back one quart of alcoholic beverages duty free. You cannot bring drugs in from Mexico, naturally, and unless you have a permit to do so, you cannot bring back any plants or vegetables.

At the risk of spoiling it, I'm going to tell you that I've found that the border station at Tecate is much less troublesome to get through then the one at Tijuana. There's less traffic at Tecate, for one thing, and the border guards behave more like human beings than short-tempered automatons.

At Tijuana the formalities include a computer check of license plate numbers and occasionally a thorough inspection in the big shed where you may get a mirror run under your car and even specially trained dogs sniffing for traces of drugs.

Unfortunately, getting back into the U.S. is almost always the most tedious and least pleasant formality the Baja traveler has to undergo. I can't explain it except that it does inform you in an unmistakable way that the freedom you've enjoyed in Baja is over and that you're back in the land of the great no-no.

Books, Guide & Otherwise

FOR A PLACE that has been so far off the beaten track and so little visited by the masses, there has been a amazing number of books written about Baja California. It's almost as if everyone who ever went there wrote a book about it. As you'd expect, the quality varies considerably but just about all of the books are worth reading, even the worst.

The one book for the off-pavement Baja motorist not to be without is *Lower California Guidebook* by Peter Gerhard and Howard E. Gulick (Arthur H. Clark Co., Glendale, Calif.). A page from G&G has been reproduced on the next page to give you an idea how detailed and how complete this book is. It is in the form of a road log but also includes historical notes, and information on interesting plants and geological formations. With information like this, you can have the confidence you need to go just about anywhere in Baja.

It was originally published in 1956, revised in 1958, revised again in 1962, then brought up to date with a chapter of notes for the fourth edition in 1967. Only a few years ago literally every building in Baja was noted in their guide and when they said there would be an abandoned rancho on the right just before the dry stream bed, you could depend on it. With the coming of the pavement and the many other changes taking place in Baja, the information about the main road is of course out of date. That really doesn't matter, however, because the information about the country, its history, the flora and the geology is still valid. More important for the off-pavement motorist is the fact that the side roads, by-roads and trails they wrote about are still very much as they were then. Sure, you do have to make some allowances for change, even on the side roads, but the basic features are still there and in many places things are so much the same that they might have written the book last week.

So *Lower California Guidebook* is the basic book. It is widely available in southern California bookstores as well as several good mail order sources (see "Sources" at the back of the book).

For the off-pavement motorist, the best Baja maps are also included in *Lower California Guidebook*. Like the text, they are not

---

156   LOWER CALIFORNIA GUIDEBOOK

Mi. from Loreto	Partial Mileage	
17.7	(1.0)	Side road goes via SAN PUERTA VIEJA (ranch 10.4 mi.), a grade (summit 13.4 mi. from junction), and LLANO DE SAN JULIO (dry lake, 21.7 mi.) to SAN JOSÉ DE COMONDÚ (28.2 mi. from junction, see pp. 157-58).
19.3	(1.6)	EL HORNO. Cattle ranch.
22.2	(2.9)	SAN JAVIER. Elev. 1,020 ft. A small agricultural settlement

dependent upon a tiny spring ½ mile above the town, which is used to irrigate several acres of fruit trees and vegetables. The mission of San Francisco Javier de Vigge was first founded at Rancho Viejo in 1699 by Padre Francisco María Piccolo, S.J. The present site was developed as a visiting station and garden by Padre Juan de Ugarte in 1707, and the mission headquarters was moved here about 1720.

The impressive stone church, of simple Moorish style, was begun in 1744 and finished in 1758. It is the best-preserved and finest Jesuit church in Baja California. To the left of the entrance is a baptistry, and to the right a spiral staircase to the choir loft and bell tower. Two of the bells bear the date of 1761, and the third 1803. The stone work and ornamentation is remarkable. There are two small lateral chapels. The gilded *altar mayor* with its statue of St. Francis was brought in 32 boxes from Mexico City. Behind the altar are four large rooms arranged in two stories, and off to one side are two more rooms intended for missionaries' quarters. Behind the church are extensive gardens and two stone reservoirs built by the Jesuits and still in use. Above looms a great black cliff dwarfing the tiny settlement (see illustration p. 163).

The houses are arranged in two neat rows before the church and between the dry arroyo and a single irrigation ditch. There are many kinds of fruit trees, but the chief harvest is of olives. There are several venerable old olive trees said to have been planted from seed by the Jesuits.

On the Saint's feast day (December 3) hundreds of ranchers come to San Javier, some of them traveling a week or more on muleback across rough mountain trails.

The road continues down Arroyo Santo Domingo:

	Partial Mileage	
23.6	(1.4)	SEGUNDO PASO. Ranch.
24.7	(1.1)	EL RANCHITO. Trail left to LOS DOLORES (1.5 mi.), formerly a visiting station of San Javier mission, now a small agricultural center producing wheat and figs.
26.9	(2.2)	PRESA VIEJA. Cattle ranch.
28.8	(1.9)	AGUA ESCONDIDA. Cattle ranch and garden.
32.5	(3.7)	SANTO DOMINGO. A pool of water surrounded by fan palms.
33.3	(0.8)	LA PRESENTACIÓN (uninhabited). Off the road to the right are the ruins of a stone chapel and a large stone reservoir, probably built by the Franciscan Fr. Palou about 1769.
35.3	(2.0)	POZA DE TERESA. Ranch.
41.2	(5.9)	PALO BLANCO. Ranch.
48.8	(7.6)	SAN IGNACIO. Cattle ranch.

Gerhard & Gulick. Gives you the confidence to go anywhere.

up to date so far as the main road goes but they're still better than anything else that's available. These maps are printed in handy, detailed sections rather than one large map, and while a pamphlet of G&G maps is available separately, I find it far handier to use those in the book.

Curiously, the best, most up-to-date road map of Baja at the present time is one that is produced for private pilots who fly in Baja. This is Arnold Senterfitt's *Complete Chart of Baja California,* and while its primary purpose is to pinpoint every one of the 146 landing strips in Baja, it also shows roads and trails and can be very helpful because it is kept up to date where other maps are not. Senterfitt has a companion book that goes with the map, *Airports of Baja California,* and this, in addition to being invaluable to the pilot in Baja, is also of considerable interest to the earth-bound driver because of the carefully done notes.

There's also a special map you should know about. This is based on Gerhard and Gulick's guidebook but has later information incorporated into it as well. This is put out by Mike McMahan, another old Baja hand, and is available in black and white, in color, and in color with a plastic coat over it. It is too large to be used conveniently while traveling, however, unless it is cut up into sections. It makes a handsome wall decoration, though, and it seems to me that most Baja buffs have one.

Because Gerhard and Gulick's *Lower California Handbook* is so good, it makes almost all the other guidebooks to Baja unnecessary. Most of the other guides concentrated almost exclusively on the old main route from Ensenada to La Paz and are, as a consequence, of little more than background value for the Baja traveler today. Also, as a perhaps unfair generalization, most of them leaned heavily on G&G for information about side roads and lesser-traveled routes and are consequently pretty secondhand. Nevertheless, these other guides are worth reading simply because everyone who goes to Baja sees things a little differently and any of them may open your eyes to something you might not otherwise be aware of.

A couple of the more recent books of this type that you may find worth looking at include the *Sunset Travel Guide to Baja California,* by Ken and Caroline Bates (Lane Books, Menlo Park, California) and the even newer Life book, *Baja California,* by William Weber (Time-Life Books, Chicago, 1973).

The Automobile Club of Southern California has guidebooks and a map that are available to their members or members of clubs affiliated with the American Automobile Association. Some years ago the auto club guide was the only one available for Baja but this was in a simpler time when the club was interested in encouraging motoring as an adventure and had not settled down to its conservative middle age in which it is primarily concerned with selling insurance, financing cars and running a travel agency.

The auto club revises their map of Baja periodically and while many of the side roads on which you may want to travel are simply not shown at all, it is good for the main road and as a general reference.

The club's guides (one for the northern half, another for the southern) are also revised from time to time and their greatest value is for information about hotels and motels.

There's a series of small books published by a gentleman in Glendale, California, named Walt Wheelock that are worth knowing about. Walt is an old Baja hand whose specialty is *La Frontera,* the northern part of the peninsula, and his La Siesta Press has published more good stuff about this part of Baja than any other.

There are four guidebooks from La Siesta and though some of the information is no longer pertinent because of the changes on the peninsula in the past few years, all are worth reading. These are *Baja California Overland,* by L. Burr Belden (1967), *Camping and Climbing in Baja,* by John W. Robinson (1967), plus two by Walt Wheelock himself, *Beaches of Baja,* (1968) and *Byroads of Baja* (1971).

In addition, La Siesta has published three valuable background books. *Palm Canyons of Baja California,* by Randall Henderson (1971) is made up of reprints of articles that originally appeared in *Desert Magazine* when Henderson was exploring the palm canyons near the Laguna Salada shortly after World War II. *Flora of Baja Norte,* by Tina Kasbeer (1971), contains good historical notes about the botanists that worked in Baja in the early days plus listings of the more common plants you'll see. My only regret is that there aren't drawings and photos of the plants. And there's *Towns of Baja California,* by David Goldbaum (1971). This book, which has notes by William O. Hendricks, is a 1918 report from Goldbaum to the Mexican government about the towns in the northern part of the peninsula and Hendricks' notes add a scholarly update from other sources. If you get involved with Baja, you'll want all of the La Siesta books.

Then come those books that are just plain fun to read. First on my list is *Forgotten Peninsula,* by Joseph Wood Krutch (William Sloan Associates, New York, 1961). Professor Krutch, a most civilized man, traveled widely in Baja by car, plane and mule-back before putting this book together. Although the trips he describes were made in the 1950s, his observations and descriptions are still largely accurate and consistently pertinent even though some of the details have changed. Although the hardbound edition is now out of print, an Apollo paperback was made available later.

Excerpts from *Forgotten Peninsula* were also used in the spectacular *Baja California, Geography of Hope,* with photographs by Elliot Porter (Sierra Club, San Francisco, 1968) and in a less expensive paperback edition (Ballantine Books, New York, 1969).

Journey of the Flame, by Antonio de Fierro Blanco (Houghton Mifflin Co., Cambridge, Massachusetts, 1933), stands with Krutch as my favorite book about Baja. This was written by Walter Nordhoff (under whose name it may be found instead of the pseudonym), the father of Charles Nordhoff, co-author of *Mutiny on the Bounty.* This was a best seller when it was published 30 years ago and it is a tribute to its quality that it has been re-issued several times by the publisher. Although it is a novel—a story told by an old man of a journey he made up the peninsula when he was a boy—it is fascinating because of its interweaving of historical fact with the legends of the Peninsula.

Erle Stanley Gardner wrote several books about Baja and they are all fun to read. Gardner, the prolific creator of the Perry Mason mysteries, was a desert buff and a Baja buff. His books are not of great direct value to the traveler since they are accounts of expeditions he made into Baja rather than guidebooks. Unlike most Baja books, you're likely to find Gardner's in your public library. The titles, all published by Morrow, New York, are *Land of Shorter Shadows* (1948), *Hunting the Desert Whale* (1960), *Hovering over Baja* (1961), *Hidden Heart of Baja* (1962), *Off the Beaten Path in Baja* (1967), *Mexico's Magic Square* (1968), *Host with a Big Hat* (1969). I hope I haven't forgotten any.

There have been a number of books written about personal experiences in Baja and almost any of these that you can find are worth reading. Among those I've enjoyed are *Land Where Time Stands Still,* by Max Miller (Dodd, Mead and Co., New York, 1943); *Baja California: Hunting, Fishing and Travel in Lower California,* by Ralph Hancock and friends (Academy Publishers, Los Angeles, 1953); *Bouncing Down to Baja,* by Orv and Bill Wortman (Westernlore Press, Los Angeles, 1959); *Mexico's Diamond in the Rough,* by O.W. Timberman (Westernlore Press, Los Angeles, 1959) and *There it is: Baja,* by Mike McMahan (Manessier Publishing, Riverside, California, 1973).

Much historical information has been generated about Baja over the years and some of those you might find interesting for background are:

Observations in Lower California, by Johan Jakob Baegert (University of California Press, Berkeley and Los Angeles, 1952). Father Baegert, a Jesuit missionary, was stationed at Mission San Luis Gonzaga from 1751 to 1768 and his description of life in Baja and of the primitive tribes of the area reveals much, not only about the Indians and the country, but also about the missionaries who were there to make Christians of them.

History of Lower California, by F.J. Clavigero (Stanford University Press, Palo Alto, California, 1937). A history of the Jesuit period originally published in 1789.

Black Robes in Lower California, by P.M. Dunne (University of California Press, Berkeley and Los Angeles, 1952). A history of the Jesuit period with good material on the early padres.

As you read more and more about Baja, you'll become something of an expert on your own. And this is fun too. I'll never forget, for instance, the satisfaction I received on finding a mistake in a world atlas that put Santa Catarina where San Agustin should have been.

It's also fun to run across things about Baja in unexpected places. As in a book about the California gold rush called *Six Months in the Gold Mines,* by E. Gould Buffum, where a chapter on La Paz was included because the author spent a year there as a lieutenant in the U.S. army when La Paz was occupied during the Mexican war of 1846-48. Or in the biography of the boxer Jack Johnson, *Black Champion,* by Finis Farr, in which a story is told about Jack and his party finding themselves aboard a boat in the Gulf of California carrying Chinese laborers that were being smuggled into the U.S. Or when reading about the American filibusterer, William Walker, and discovering that while his more famous exploits took place in Nicaragua, he also had a fling in Baja in 1853. Or that another group of Americans assisted in the revolution in northern Baja in 1911, creating all sorts of embarrassment for the U.S. government. It's a fascinating place to read about.

There's one special source for Baja books that deserves to be mentioned and this is Dawson's Book Shop in Los Angeles (see "Sources"). They not only carry as near a complete line of current Baja books as anyone I know but also have many that are not available elsewhere. Dawson's also publishes a Baja California Travel Series that the serious Baja buff should be aware of. You can get information about these by writing them.

What Kinds of Vehicles Go to Baja?

WHAT KINDS of vehicles go to Baja? All kinds, all kinds—cars, station wagons, trucks, buses, buggies, bikes and Broncos. It al depends on how fast you want to go, where you want to go and how you want to live while you're there. But since we're talking about going to the *real* Baja, which lies off the pavement and may be on a trail that can only be described as primitive, maybe we'd better talk about vehicles a little.

DUNE BUGGY

The quickest way to cover the ground in the real Baja (assuming you're not going on a motorcycle) is probably by dune buggy. These machines, usually open-bodies roadsters on shortened Volkswagen chassis, have many advantages. First, because they are light, have supple suspension and are extremely maneuverable, they are comfortable to ride in at comparatively high speeds, even on bad roads. You can cover the ground and do it quickly.

The main disadvantage, as far as I'm concerned, is that they offer too little opportunity for those little extras that can make off-pavement travel more pleasant. The luggage space is minimal, for example, so the buggista is pretty well restricted to the bare necessities. In addition, the occupants get awfully dirty awfully fast in the typical buggy and while you can get used to this—or at least tolerate it for a few days until you can get a bath—it doesn't add much to the enchantment of the journey.

FOUR WHEEL DRIVE

You probably don't really need 4-wheel drive to go to even the real Baja. Nevertheless, a 4wd is the kind of vehical that is most likely to give you the freedom from anxiety that can make your trip more pleasant. With 4-wheel drive and a bit of skill, you can go just about anyplace in Baja. It's still possible to get stuck, of course, but your chances of making it through without drama are far better than in anything else.

The specific advantages of 4wd are numerous. Because it is expected to get hard use, a 4wd vehicle is built to stand up to the

What kinds of vehicles go to Baja? Broncos (heavily laden)...

rigors of off-pavement travel. Consequently, it's far less likely to shed a vital part at some inopportune moment. The 4wd feature itself is also extremely practical because you then have *traccion doble,* as the Mexicans say. You also have a set of low-range gears in the transfer case of most 4wds, which is just the thing you need when the grade is steep and the going is slow—as it often is in Baja.

The modern 4wd vehicle, unlike those of only a few years ago, can be a pretty civilized machine. You can motor about in comfort, even in luxury, if your pocketbook and tastes extend to that sort of thing. You have a very wide choice in 4wd machines, everything from a basic, open-topped CJ5 to an all-out luxury station wagon from Jeep, Chevrolet or International with power steering, power brakes, automatic transmission and air conditioning. And don't sneer at air conditioning, it's a good thing to have in Baja. Not because you need refrigerated air, usually, but because it enables you to close the vehicle up tight to keep the dust out and still be comfortable. My wife, who has been there both ways, says air conditioning makes the difference between *endure* and *enjoy*.

The disadvantages of a 4wd are mostly financial. They are specialized machines and you pay quite a lot for that. Off the pavement their comparatively crude design (solid axles front and rear, no suspension travel to speak of) makes them far less comfortable than a dune buggy, given equal speeds; and on the highway, no matter what anybody tries to tell you, it's not like driving a family sedan.

Big 4-wheel drive campers weighing as much as four tons...

If you're seriously considering a 4wd machine, or if you already have one but don't feel you qualify as an expert, you may find a small book called *Four Wheel Drive Handbook* (Bond/Parkhurst Publications, Newport Beach, California) of value. And, oh yes, I was the co-author of that book, in case that might influence your decision.

TWO-WHEEL DRIVE

There's nothing wrong with using a 2-wheel-drive vehicle for your off-pavement adventuring in Baja. How satisfactory it is depends almost entirely on the skill of the driver.

This may be an oversimplification. Perhaps a couple qualifications should be added since, in addition to a skillful driver, you also honestly need a useful quantity of ground clearance and a limited-slip differential. It would also be helpful to have oversize tires to help you through the sand you encounter.

The most common 2wd seen in the real Baja is the standard pickup truck. You see many of these and while they perhaps won't go everyplace a 4wd might, they obviously get along very well—especially if they have an extra-low first gear to use for creeping when that's the wise thing to do.

The Volkswagen bus is also a highly satisfactory Baja transporter. It is short, nimble and has excellent traction characteristics. I've never traveled Baja in a VW bus but from the number of them you encounter, it has to be pretty well suited.

A trimmed Volkswagen Beetle with a "Baja Bug" kit bolted on...

I wouldn't recommend taking a family sedan or station wagon very far off the pavement in Baja unless it were specially prepared for such travel with extra ground clearance, limited slip, big tires and skid plates in the appropriate places to protect the tenderest parts of the underneath side.

PICKUP CAMPERS

Pickup campers, both 2wd and 4wd, are traveling in Baja these days. Personally, however, as much as a fully laden 10- or 12-ft camper rig weighs, I'd be a little hesitant about getting too far away from the paved road with anything less than 4wd. Of course there are many good side roads where such a 2wd camper could go with impunity, but I wouldn't suggest being intrepid about exploring dim tracks.

Pickup trucks that are properly prepared to carry a camper already have heavy duty springs, extra strong tires, etc., so it wouldn't require a lot of preparation for a Baja journey. Limited-slip would be advisable, as would skid plates, but that should be sufficient.

In a camper you will have to travel at a very moderate pace

And even tiny 360-cc Japanese Cony pickup trucks go to Baja.

compared to a dune buggy or 4wd but because you don't have to spend two or three hours a day making and breaking camp, you can add at least that many more hours of travel to your day. I never feel like I'd like to change places with a camper when I see one inching along the trail but I do admit a twinge of envy when I'm still unfolding my tent while the camper driver has had to do nothing more than level up his rig before settling down with a cool drink to enjoy the evening air.

VANS & MOTOR HOMES

Because there's so much difference in weight and size between a compact van and a full-scale motorhome, it's difficult to generalize about their suitability for Baja travel. Unless you're a skilled, experienced rough-country driver, I'd suggest sticking to the better-traveled side roads and leave the more serious exploring to the smaller vehicles. This isn't to say that a van or a small motorhome can't go to a lot of beautiful places in Baja; there are certainly plenty of worthwhile sights that you can reach without trouble.

Sand is going to be your most common hazard with such a vehicle since even the "good" side roads often traverse the occasional wash. So do be prepared to get yourself unstuck if you get bogged in the dreaded sand.

TRAILERS

Before the pavement was in, I would have advised against taking a trailer to Baja. Now, however, if you've a mind to do it, there's no reason you can't tow your travel trailer down the highway. There are already some trailer parks established in the spectacular Conception Bay area and there will no doubt be more in the near future. You won't see much of the real Baja that way but if you were to do your towing with a big 4wd vehicle, use the trailer as a base of operations and the 4wd for your serious side trips, it could work out beautifully.

Getting Ready Takes Only Common Sense

GETTING READY for a trip off the pavement in Baja is pretty much a matter of common sense. It's primitive country you're going into and the wisest traveler is the one that's best prepared. The vehicle should be in good shape to start with, it should be equipped with seat belts to keep you from rattling around, the tires should be good, you should carry the equipment necessary to get yourself out if you get stuck and you should have some basic tools and spare parts in case you need to make repairs along the way. You should also be sure to have enough food and water to see you through in case you do become inextricably bogged or your machine breaks down and you don't have the necessary parts, tools, or skill to effect a repair.

CAR PREPARATION

You should first of all be sure the vehicle is in shape to make the trip. This means having the drive train and running gear just as sound as it can be made. Radiator and heater line hoses should be checked and replaced if there's any sign of deterioration such as cracks, checks, or worn spots. Battery cables should be examined and the battery itself be in such a condition that its durability is above suspicion. Shock absorbers should be given careful scrutiny, not only for leaks but for function as well.

The points and plugs should be new or as good as new, the air filter clean, the in-line fuel filter likewise and all drive belts should be without any evidence of wear or deterioration. If there's anything loose it should be thoroughly tightened and you should get a chassis lube and an oil change, if not a complete tune-up, before shoving off.

This is all basic stuff you'd no doubt think of without my help but they are important enough to be put on a check list just to make sure nothing has been overlooked.

TIRES

There's no doubt at all that one of the main concerns of the side-road traveler in Baja is his tires. I don't pretend to be an expert about tires, but I do have some generalities to offer, so let's see if I can tell you anything you need to know.

For a conventional 2- or 4-wheel-drive machine—not a lightweight buggy or a heavyweight camper—I'd recommend nothing less than full 4-ply tires in as-new condition. Judging by the number of brand new rigs now seen in Baja, I'd say you're probably typical if you make your first Baja trip on the tires that came on the vehicle from the factory. If these are standard size or slightly larger than standard, they'll probably see you through at least one good hard trip without anything more serious than an occasional puncture. Don't expect anything like "normal" mileage out of these tires, though, as the abuse they take from rocks and ruts is very likely to result in blowouts from cord fatigue long before the tread has disappeared.

Honestly, for use in Baja, there isn't any worthwhile difference between a conventional highway tread pattern and one with a mud-and-snow design. Admittedly, the mud-and-snow tread looks like a much more serious tire but its benefits are almost wholly psychological as the carcass is not stronger and the tread doesn't actually contain any more rubber than a conventional tread. In good, slick mud a cleated tire does have some benefit since it will tear into the surface and maybe get a grip that a smoother tire couldn't achieve, but mud isn't a problem you ordinarily face in Baja. Sand is a much more common Baja hazard and in sand it's possible to demonstrate that a tire with a smooth tread has an advantage over one with a rough tread since it is far less likely to tear the delicate surface and dig in. More important than tread design, so far as traction in sand is concerned, is inflation pressure. A tire that is soft enough to conform to the surface it encounters will develop far more traction than even the most aggressive tread at a full-up, normal inflation pressure.

All things considered, I think the best advice is to consult somebody whose business it is to know about the tires that are suitable for your vehicle. Along this line, the best source for information I know is Dick Cepek (see "Sources"). Dick is an old Baja hand as well as a widely experienced tire man and gets lots of feedback from the users of all makes of tires.

If you're going to put new tires on your machine before going to Baja, I'd suggest using as big a standard-size tire as possible without going to the super-fat sand tires that quickly run the price up and aren't really all that necessary for the Baja traveler.

Again, still talking about a conventional 2wd or 4wd, I'd suggest that an L78-15 or a 9.15-15 is as wide a tire as you really need for Baja. But be sure to mount them on rims that are appropriately wide as you'll otherwise end up with a squirrely handling vehicle on the highway and still not get the maximum benefit from their width when you're off the pavement. Conversely, don't use extra-wide rims with a narrow tire; that makes the sidewalls even more vulnerable to stone damage.

On my own vehicles, the most satisfactory all-around combination I've found is L78-15 Armstrong Norseman tires on 8-inch rims. I've bought over a dozen of these from Dick Cepek now and have never had a bad experience with them. Sure, I've gotten stuck and I've had my share of flats but all in all I think I've had less tire trouble than most Baja motorists.

There's one other thing you might consider. If your vehicle doesn't have power steering, you'll find that the more open tread of the mud-and-snow tire requires less steering effort than a comparable tire with highway tread since it doesn't put as much bare rubber in contact with the pavement. There's no problem when you're off in the dirt but on the street it can make a big difference.

If yours is a special type of vehicle, either very light or very heavy, then you should go to tires that are adequate for the job you're going to ask of them. For a typical dune buggy the accepted Baja practice is to use a stock size wheel and tire in front to keep it easy to steer and use larger wheels and tires on the rear. Not too large, though, as this reduces the amount of torque that can be effectively delivered and too wide a tire begins to reach out to the sides of the narrow track for those sharp rocks.

For the pickup camper, where the rear tires can be carrying up to 2500-3000 pounds each, the only intelligent solution is to go to 6-, 8-, or 10-ply tires that are strong enough to carry the load. Don't plan on running dual wheels on your vehicle very far off the pavement, though, it just isn't practical because of the narrow ruts you often have to follow. Even the biggest supply trucks that travel the side roads in Baja use single-tire set-ups on the rear for this reason.

On any serious trip into Baja, I'd recommend carrying two spare tires; especially if you don't plan on fixing your own flats. This gives you a reasonable margin for bad luck and if you also carry an extra tube you can generally find someone who can help you with it even if you don't have the necessary equipment to de-mount and re-mount the tire.

We'll get into some more tire lore later on concerning pressures, etc., but this should give you an idea of the tires you'll need on your Baja expedition.

DE-DITCHING GEAR

Sand is the hazard most likely to bring the traveler to an unscheduled stop off the pavement in Baja. So it's just as well to face up to the fact that you're going to encounter at least some deep sand or silt and be prepared for it.

Once you are stuck in sand, there are four basic things required to get you out. You'll need a jack, a pair of sand mats, a shovel, and patience. For the greatest efficiency, the jack should be a tall bumper jack and the best of these is a Hi-Lift. If you don't opt for the Hi-Lift (about $30), at least be sure that your jack is strong and durable. Don't depend on the factory-furnished bumper jack that came with the car. It will almost certainly let you down when you need it most. Also be sure to have a board at least a foot square that you can use as a jack pad under the base to keep the jack from disappearing into the sand.

With a good jack to lift the car, a shovel to scoop out with, something solid to put under the tires (boards, industrial belting, etc.) and lots of patience, you can get through all but the most hopeless sand traps. If, in addition, you have a good strong tow chain, you may be able to get a helpful pull.

TOOLS & SPARE PARTS

A basic toolbox is a necessity for the Baja traveler and while this need not be elaborate, it should include at least a set of open-end wrenches (up to about 1-¼ inches), a 2-inch crescent wrench, hacksaw (or at least a hacksaw blade), tire gauge, hammer, pliers and a couple screwdrivers. Another tool not to be forgotten is a lug wrench. Not the flimsy one that came with the car but a better one from the auto supply store. There is almost nothing as frustrating having a jack that won't or a lug wrench that gives up just when it's needed most.

As for spare parts, I'd say take along everything you can think of. Not all Baja travelers agree with me about this; I know some who roam the whole peninsula with no more spares than they can put in the glove box. They obviously enjoy tempting fate. I don't. I subscribe to the philosophy that says that if you have a spare part for it, it won't break.

The basic spares I'd suggest carrying include a fuel pump, or at least a pump repair kit, a tune-up kit (points, rotor, condenser), extra sparkplug, extra tube (even if you have tubeless tires), extra fan belt (plus any accessory drive belts your vehicle may have). I'd also recommend taking engine oil, transmission fluid, friction tape, a can of radiator stop leak, a batch of assorted nuts, bolts and washers, a hank of baling wire and a few feet of 18-gauge electrical wire. And don't forget to have an extra set of keys along.

Certainly it would add to your own feeling a self-sufficiency if you were able to repair a punctured tire, or put a tube into a tubeless one that didn't respond to plugging from outside. Because gas tanks and oil pans do sometimes get banged, a tank sealer kit is a wise thing to carry. Because epoxy can be used to repair almost anything, a small 2-tube epoxy kit is worth taking along.

If you'll excuse another plug for *Four Wheel Drive Handbook,* I'll just add that in it we include what we consider a "Peace of Mind Kit" of spare parts and accessories, plus chapters on getting unstuck and troubleshooting the most common maladies likely to afflict the off-pavement driver. If you're not an expert in such things, it might not be a bad idea to read it and take a copy along in case you ever come to the point where it might be helpful.

GASOLINE

With all the traffic there is on the main road these days, gas pumps are springing up faster than boojum trees, so the main road traveler doesn't really have any worries on this score. If you're going to get off the pavement, though, don't fall into the trap of thinking there's gasoline available at every name you see on the map.

So plot your off-pavement motoring with care, being sure that you have sufficient fuel to see you through to the next source of supply. Also keep in mind that when you get off the pavement your fuel consumption is going to increase, perhaps as much as 100 percent, so just because you were getting 14 miles to the gallon on the pavement, don't assume you can do that well in the rough.

OTHER EQUIPMENT

We'll get into a discussion of emergencies and emergency equipment later but as such items should be considered as a part of the vehicle, just let me say here that common sense requires that you carry extra water, enough food to see you through a serious delay caused by a breakdown or getting hopelessly stuck, and a first aid kit. Like the other basic items, these should be included on your check list to make sure they're not overlooked or forgotten.

What It's Like, Traveling in Baja

OR ANY OF US, if we know more or less what we're going to encounter, it's a lot easier to take that first step into a new adventure. In this chapter we're going to talk a little about what it's like to travel off the pavement— and if you're committed to seeing the real Baja, you're going to have to get off the pavement.

Nevertheless, you're going to have to spend some time getting to the place where you can get off the pavement. First, for example, you have to cross the border into Mexico and this is always a little adventure in itself.

As you drive up to the border station, which looks like a tollgate, you simply do what everybody else is doing; creep along, looking at the guard. If he doesn't make any sign for you to stop, and he most likely won't, you simply motor on through. If he chooses, to, he may ask you what you're carrying in your vehicle or where you're going, then wave you on. Or he might even tell you to park over there and report to the *aduana* (customs) office, but that is unlikely unless you look like you're carrying commercial goods. Only a few years ago the border officials discouraged people with long hair from entering Mexico but that no longer seems to be true.

After you've crossed the border, the first order of business, assuming you didn't take care of it earlier, is your car insurance. You'll see signs for the various agencies, often accompanied by curb-side helpers who will encourage you to patronize their establishment.

Before leaving the tourist zone near the border (Ensenada on the Pacific side, San Felipe on the Gulf), you will probably want to stop and get the last-minute supplies that all Baja travelers seem to require. A visit to the *panaderia* (bakery), for example, where you can get delicious fresh rolls which will remain palatable for several days if they're kept in air-tight plastic bags.

You should also stock up on booze before going beyond Ensenada or San Felipe since liquor stores become non-existent for a distance of several hundred miles to the south. You can get beer in the smaller places but the government is attempting to colonize the peninsula

with sober, hard-working people and therefore does not permit the sale of liquor except in resort areas that cater to the tourist trade or in the industrial towns such as Guerrero Negro.

Tequila is the national liquor of Mexico and the better brands (Cuervo Especial is a particular favorite) run less than $2.50 a quart. Mexican gin and vodka are also low-priced but a familiar looking label is no guarantee that it will taste exactly like the same brand sold in the States. Waterfill and Frazier opened a bourbon distillery in Mexico during prohibition and turn out a palatable, reasonably priced American-style whiskey, but scotch, rye, American bourbon and other liquors that must be imported are little cheaper than at home. Liqueurs are relatively cheap and kahlua, a very good coffee-flavored liqueur, is probably the traveler's favorite. A good Mexican brandy is named El Presidente but it isn't any less expensive than a comparable domestic brandy in the U.S. There is a variety of local wines but these are neither very cheap nor very good, being comparable to Algerian wine in case you're a connoisseur of such things. Mexican beer is excellent and comes in a variety of types, so if you don't already have a favorite you should shop around until you find the one that suits you best. Mexican beer, formerly cheap, is now slightly more expensive than American beer in the U.S.

One of the most practical drinks for the off-pavement traveler is sangrita. This is a peppers-and-tomato concoction that goes very well mixed one-to-one with tequila and is drunk without ice. It is hot, though, and you may have to be very moderate with it to avoid the dreaded Mexican heartburn.

If you're going south of Ensenada or San Felipe, you will need a tourist permit. If you enter through Mexicali or Tecate, you stop at the border station office to take care of this formality. If you're going through Ensenada, you drive on south through the town of Maneadero and stop at the *migracion* station for your permit.

For the moment, let's assume that you've already decided where you want to go and that you've arrived at the place where you're going to leave the pavement. We'll get into some "where to go" lore later on but in this chapter we're going to stick to generalities that apply to your off-pavement travels wherever you decide to go in Baja.

As soon as I drive off the pavement, I stop and do two things. First, I lock the front hubs so all it takes to put my vehicle into 4-wheel drive is a tug at the transfer case handle. Second, I lower the tire pressures. As a rule of thumb, I lower the pressures to about two-thirds of the maximum. An ordinary 4-ply tire will have a maximum inflation pressure of 32 psi, so about 20-22 is what I aim for. This is a good compromise for off-pavement running, yet not so soft that it has to be immediately pumped up again when the pavement reappears.

Letting some of the air out of the tires is mainly done for comfort since a softer tire will absorb a lot more of the road's minor irregularities and consequently reduce the jarring and rattling. A softer tire is also better in conditions of reduced traction as it is more flexible and therefore gets a better grip. Such a tire is also less resistant to impact damage but you shouldn't have any worries about jamming a rock through the casing if you stick to the

At Rancho Santa Inez, the laundry is done in the time-honored way.

two-thirds-maximum rule and don't try for any speed records.

Tire pressures also depend on the weight the tires are carrying, so with a lightweight buggy you may go down to only 8-10 psi and still have a safe margin. Conversely, with a heavy rig, you may still be carrying 35-40 psi to keep a safe margin.

Once you leave the pavement you'll begin to notice the dust and this will be your very nearly constant companion for the balance of your off-pavement travels in Baja. If your vehicle is air conditioned, dust is not a serious problem since you can simply roll up the windows, turn on the air and ignore it.

Before we had an air conditioned vehicle, the best solution we found for dust and heat was to use Sidles shades (see "Sources") on the windows to keep the sun out and turn on a pair of old-fashioned defroster fans I bought from J.C. Whitney to create a cooling breeze. This was highly satisfactory as long as the temperatures were moderate.

Unless it is so hot that you can't stand it with the windows closed, by all means keep everything, absolutely everything, sealed up tight. If you crack a window to get a little cooling air, the wind blowing across the opening creates a negative pressure in the rest of the vehicle and sucks in dust at every crack. In that case, it's better to simply open everything up and let the breeze blow through. You won't get much dirtier and you'll be a lot more comfortable.

Depending on the design of your vehicle and how tightly all the doors fit, you may also find it worthwhile to use masking tape to seal off certain cracks. When we had our Bronco we routinely sealed the cracks around the tailgate and while this was tiresome to have to do

El Marmol. Quiet now but several hundred people once lived here.

every time we opened the back end, it was worth it for the comparatively dust-free environment we could then enjoy.

If you have an open vehicle, like a dune buggy or an open-topped jeep, you're simply going to have to live with the dust and that, admittedly, can get pretty tiresome. All you can do in that case is protect those things that need it most, like cameras, for instance, with plastic bags and accept the dust as being part of the price.

It shouldn't be necessary to do anything special to the vehicle's engine for ordinary off-pavement motoring since almost all contemporary cars and trucks have good air cleaners and reasonably dust-proof ignition systems. A coating of dust followed by a heavy dew can create ignition problems, though, but removing the distributor cap and cleaning everything with a dry cloth will usually get you on your way again.

If you are not an experienced off-pavement driver, the best approach is to start out with a certain degree of caution and travel at a very moderate pace until you get the feel of the vehicle in this kind of terrain. The speed at which you'll cover the ground in Baja is dependent on the terrain and the kind of vehicle you're in. In a dune buggy, rolling right along, you may average 25-35 mph all day long. In a 4-wheel-drive vehicle, you'll go a bit slower, maybe 15-25. And in a pickup with a camper on the back, you'll go slower than that on the average unpaved road. These estimates may be a little high for a full day's run since your daily average depends a lot on how many stops you make to take pictures, drink beer, or just appreciate the country. I consider 75-100 miles a day plenty fast enough in Baja, and I know that the slower you go the more you'll see of the country.

One of the sources of concern for the off-pavement motorist in Baja is gasoline. With the new highway down the length of the peninsula, gasoline isn't the concern it once was since there must now be no more than 50 miles between dependable sources. Off the pavement, however, you can't depend on there being a gas station there when you need it and for this reason a certain amount of caution is advised. The wisest practice is to keep your tank well filled and always be sure you have an abundance to get you to the next source. I'd also suggest having a reserve supply just in case a "sure" source doesn't have any this week, or if you spend a lot of time getting lost, or have the misfortune to spring a leak. For instance, I always carry one 5-gallon can of gas, just to be sure, and in some really remote areas I've carried as much as 20 gallons.

There are lots of gas pumps along the main road but the time-honored way of getting gas in Baja is to buy it at a rancho that keeps a few 55-gallon drums on hand to supply the local needs. The proper procedure at such a place is to stop near the drums and wait for somebody to appear. Then you ask, *"Gasolina?"* If the response is affirmative, the next step is to remove the gas cap, smile, and say, *"Jene el tanque, por favor."*

At this the senor removes the bung from one of the barrels, takes a 6-foot length of what is usually 1-inch garden hose, inserts one end in the barrel and with a practiced suck on the hose starts the siphon action and directs it into a 5-gallon can. The 5-gallon can may be a typical U.S. army surplus can, a square can that once held anything from motor oil to fertilizer, or it may be a square can with the top cut out and a board nailed between the sides to make a handle. Once the can is full it is carried to the car and, propped up above the level of the filler cap, the gasoline is siphoned into the tank.

If it takes less than an even 5, 10 or 15 gallons to fill your tank, a calibrated stick is inserted into the can and the amount left over is deducted from the total.

The production of gasoline in Mexico is a government-owned industry, the petroleum interests that were confiscated in 1938 being nationalized for that purpose. Called Petroleos Mexicanos, or Pemex, it comes in three grades—100 octane (the orange or yellow pump), 90 octane (green pump) and 80 octane (red pump). At the small ranchos, however, there is only one grade and in my experience you get 90 octane, usually, but occasionally get the 80.

If your vehicle has a compression ratio of about 8.5:1 or lower, you can usually run 90 octane with no trouble except for a bit of pinging. But 80 octane in the same engine will ping and clatter considerably, as well as cause the engine to chug on after the ignition is turned off. If it does this, you can stop it by turning off the ignition and giving the accelerator one or more pumps to squirt raw gas from the pump jets into the cylinders to cool the hot spots that are causing the detonation.

The price for *una lata,* one container, of gasoline can vary from about $2.00 to $3.00 these days—or 40 to 60 cents a gallon—which isn't bad considering the inconvenience of having it delivered there.

There are no restrictions on where you can camp, in case you're worried about that. There is a blessed freedom from the no-no signs that cover the ground almost anywhere you camp in the U.S., no speed limit signs, no pious exhortations about preserving our fair land, or any of the other impedimenta that are heaped on the traveler in such generous doses in the U.S. If you find a place you want to camp, do it. My only recommendation about a camping place is to get far enough from the main road that you can find wood for your campfire and not be disturbed by the traffic. When I'm camping in Baja I consider it a poor campsite if I hear a single vehicle go by during the night.

When we're going to camp overnight, we like to stop about an hour or an hour and a half before dark. This affords plenty of time to set up the camp in daylight and get everything pretty much arranged before it's time to sit and enjoy the sunset. Setting up camp after dark is no more fun in Baja than it is anyplace else.

I don't think there are any special precautions necessary regarding snakes, animals or other pests. There are people who've gone to Baja for years without seeing a rattlesnake but I'm not one of them. There are rattlers in Baja, make no mistake about it, and you would be remiss not to take the basic precaution of carrying a snake-bite kit. You should also look where you're going when you're walking, and when climbing around rocks, don't put your hand into a place you haven't looked into first to make sure it's snake-free. Your best insurance is to stamp your feet a lot as any snake is inclined to avoid confrontation with you if that's possible. You stamp your feet because snakes don't have ears but they do have good vibration detection devices.

The temperature also has much to do with how active a snake is going to be. During the cool winter weather, a snake is likely to be out moving around in the warmest part of the day. At night, or in the morning while it is still chilly, he'll be sluggish and inactive. On the other hand, when it is summer, he will lay up in the shade during the day, avoiding the burning sun, and do his hunting during the more comfortable hours of the night. In that kind of weather you should put on your shoes, carry a flashlight, and create sufficient vibrations to warn the snakes that you're coming.

There are lots of little lizards in Baja, as there are in all deserts, but

Typical vegetation in northern Baja. This was taken near Sauzalito.

these are harmless as well as being very shy.

In some camping spots, especially popular ones where travelers often stop, you may have a mouse visit your camp looking for food. These are sometimes pretty bold and will occasionally come right out in the full glare of your lantern to gather up crumbs.

There are coyotes in Baja, happily, and if you put out food for them beyond the perimeter of your camp, they'll take it. They'll come up quite close to a silent camp but are neither so brazen or insistent as the dogs or cats (or bears) in a national park. On a little-traveled sideroad you may occasionally see a coyote loping across a field or disappearing into the brush but for the most part they have learned to avoid the highway.

You can also expect there to be some insect life in Baja except during the coolest months of the year. We always try to carry an

Tall, slim plants are Boojum trees; a rare and exotic sight.

aerosol can of patio spray plus a repellant to be applied directly to the clothing. There are scorpions (usually found under a rock or the underside of a piece of rotting wood) whose sting might make you sick but won't kill you, and tarantulas, whose bite, if you could persuade one to bite you, is harmless. There are also some spiders and while I've never identified any I've seen in Baja as being poisonous, we always label them as the Dreaded Baja Tent Spider and send them on their way.

In gathering wood for your fire, you'll probably be content to collect whatever you can find. A dead boojum log, thoroughly dried, makes a hot fire and, like the cactus skeleton, burns very quickly. If you're in a wash, good firewood can often be pulled out of the drifts that have piled up in the crevices or against a tree.

Because Baja is so free of restrictions and because more and more

Dune buggy travelers stop for lunch in downtown La Purisima.

It's usually just about this quiet near the town square in Mulege.

visitors are going there, there is already a lot of unsightly litter in the form of beer cans, bottles and plastic containers. We try not to add to this and recommend carrying all non-combustible trash out with you. It isn't a good idea to bury anything as it will almost certainly be dug up and scattered by coyotes or other animals. Cans can be tossed into the fire to burn off the last traces of food, then smashed flat with an axe and carried in an empty box or gunny sack without inconvenience until you arrive at a town dump where you can leave them with a clear conscience.

We also make a practice of letting fires burn out and leaving them uncovered rather than burying them. Leaving the ashes exposed allows them to be scattered by the winds rather than captured under the sand to turn into an unsightly monument for some other traveler to exhume.

There's no reason to run short of water in Baja, especially if there are any ranches in the vicinity. The ranches all have water, otherwise they wouldn't be able to survive. The deserted ranches you see are generally deserted because their wells went dry, forcing the residents to move elsewhere. Water is precious to these people in Baja, however, and should not be wasted. Nor should the fact that there is water to be had at these places be any excuse for you not to carry ample supplies for any emergency you might encounter.

The children in Baja, though those along the highway are learning that the American traveler is an easy mark, are mostly rather quiet and shy with visitors. Like all children, they respond to small gifts, and pieces of candy are always welcome. They like having their pictures taken, usually, and will pose for you if you encourage them. If you want to make friends of them, you can do no better than to have a Polaroid camera with which you can take a picture that you can give them on the spot. Naturally, taking a Polaroid of a family is a sure way of making a hit with the parents as well as the children.

Of all the children I have seen in Baja, only those we encountered in the old mining town of El Triunfo south of La Paz seemed to be inadequately clothed and fed. These children were gaunt, their clothing ragged, their feet bare, their faces smudged with dirt and showing the unmistakable signs of not having enough to eat. Faces of children such as those can haunt you but for the most part the children in Baja are not pitiful. Their government is educating them, their hard-working families take just as good care of them as they can, they're neatly dressed, clean and delightful. They like the excitement of having strangers pass their isolated homes and on some of the lesser traveled roads they have to think about it a little while before shyly returning your wave.

Abandoned mines are worth visiting. This is Desengano near L.A. Bay.

When to Go, How Long to Stay, How Much to Spend

WHEN TO GO to Baja is perhaps the next question that needs to be answered. You could go anytime, of course, but like most specialized places, some times are better than others. How long you should stay and how much you will spend depends on still other things.

First, when to go? Baja California has a desert climate and most of the peninsula should be avoided by the average traveler during the summer months. And because it lies closer to the equator than those places where most of us live, the summer season is comparably longer than it is farther north. October is likely to be uncomfortably hot but November is generally good, so far as the temperature is concerned. So from then up through the end of April, or even mid-May, when it begins to get too hot again, is the best time for visiting Baja.

If you want to go at the absolute best time of the year, so far as the desert flora is concerned, I'd suggest mid-February through mid-April. Most of the winter chill has gone by then, the days are likely to be pleasantly warm and the nights not too chilly. More important, however, this is the season when the desert is most likely to be at its most spectacular with all the fascinating plants responding to the winter rains and the wild flowers springing up in their profusion. The larger plants don't get their blossoms this early, except for an occasional one to tantalize you, but there'll still be enough to keep your eyes full of wonder.

At this time of year you can travel comfortably almost anywhere in Baja. At any time of the year the east coast is likely to be warmer and drier than the west but by the first part of May the east side is likely to begin to sizzle in the summer heat and continue to sizzle right up to November.

On the west side near the Pacific it stays cooler longer and if you stay close to the ocean you can go there even in mid-summer without suffering too much. The beaches all along the west coast are very pleasant during the summer; in fact, the climate there is much like that in the coastal areas of Los Angeles and San Diego. Likewise, there

The old gold ore mill near Las Arrastras south of San Luis Gonzaga.

is more likely to be rain, foggy days and colder nights along this coast at any time of the year.

The season of the *chubasco* (hurricane), if there is one, occurs in late summer and early fall. These don't happen often but can be extremely violent, as they were in 1967 and then again in 1972. At these times no area of the peninsula is safe from damage, San Felipe and El Rosario having been heavily damaged in 1967 and Mexicali being flooded in 1972.

HOW LONG?

How long a visit you make to Baja will probably depend on the length of time you can spare from whatever it is you do the rest of the year. That's the way it is with most of us. Nevertheless, I'd like to suggest that for your first trip you take only a little bite of Baja and then increase your bites as your experience and appetite demand it.

If you live in Southern California, I think it would be wise to start with weekend trips in the ragged triangle between Ensenada, San Felipe and Tecate. This area doesn't have the variety of exotic vegetation that is found farther south but there is plenty to see and many fascinating places to visit. A 3-day weekend will give you a chance to get to almost anyplace in this area and afford a very nice sample of what traveling in Baja is like. Also, it isn't so remote as it is when you get off the pavement farther south, and you haven't made such a sizable commitment in case you discover that you and off-pavement Baja aren't compatible.

If you have a week for your first trip to Baja, then it would be fun to make the loop trip south from Ensenada to the junction of the San Felipe road and return north on the Gulf of California side. On such a trip as this you do get into the exotic flora with great boojum forests, lots of giant cardon and even the lovely elephant trees. Although the basic mileage on such a trip would be only 650 or so miles, there are plenty of side roads for off-pavement exploring to make it all add up to a wonderful week-long visit.

By hurrying, or fudging another day or two onto your week, you could go on south to Bahia de Los Angeles, another very pretty area in the springtime.

The more time you have, the more you can take the time to see, of course. It is probably best to do your exploration in a somewhat methodical, well planned way, starting from the north and working your way south. In general, the northern half of the peninsula is the more interesting and scenic and what I think of as the "Best of Baja" is that area south of El Rosario and north of El Arco.

That isn't to say there aren't lots of other good places on the peninsula, however. I personally have a great affection for the area south of Tecate, for example, and such spectaculars as Bahia

This little steam engine was formerly used at the Las Flores mine.

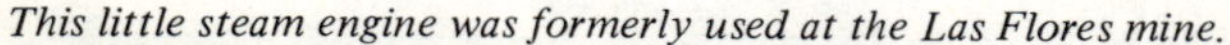

The old mission at San Javier is at the bottom of a deep valley.

Concepcion and the lump of land at the tip beyond La Paz are too beautiful to be ignored.

For a trip to La Paz, especially if you're planning any serious side-road trips, a minimum of two weeks should be allowed. If you really pushed, stopping only for fuel and to camp overnight, you could no doubt get to La Paz in two and a half days, but that isn't a trip I'd be interested in taking. If you're going to see anything, you have to go a lot slower than that. And if you want to really enjoy Baja, you should use the pavement only when there's no other way to get from here to there.

Three weeks would be a better length of time for covering the whole peninsula's length, and still there will be things you didn't have time to see. If you want to see everything it is possible to see, taking every side road that goes anyplace worth going to, you should plan on spending an entire winter at it. And that's a trip I would like to go along on.

On any trip to Baja, it always adds to the enjoyment if you plan a layover day every so often. This gives you a chance to enjoy a lazy day around camp, going for walks, or just going out into the desert and sitting, one of the most worthwhile things you can do in any desert. When you do this you begin to see birds whose presence you might not even have suspected when you were driving along the road and you also get to know and appreciate some of the more interesting plants.

On an extended trip, we like to plan a double-overnight stay every four or five days and we also like to check into a motel occasionally to shower away the accumulation of trail dust, wash out some clothes and tuck into somebody's else's cooking. It's possible to do these things in camp, too, of course, but the little touch of civilization adds a nice touch to the whole experience.

AND HOW MUCH?

It's difficult to predict exactly how much money you're likely to spend on a trip to Baja. It can be done very inexpensively or you can spend about as much as you would traveling in the U.S. If you carry all your own food and camp out all the time, your only additional expenses would be for local beer and gasoline. On the other hand, you could plan your overnight stops at the posh, fly-in type motels and pay $20-25 a day for room and board per person.

Just to have a safe margin, I plan on an average of $20 a day for shorter journeys where we won't be staying in motels and commensurately more, about $30-35 a day, for longer trips where we'll be staying in motels some of the time.

Prices are going up all over the peninsula as more and more

San Ignacio has one of the best of the old Jesuit churches.

Americans go there, as you would expect. Where the top price for gasoline in even the most remote locations was about 40 cents a gallon only a few years ago, 50 cents is far more common now and 60 cents a gallon not unusual. Supply and demand have something to do with all this, naturally, but the sharper local businessmen (and business women) are also finding that Americans will pay almost any price that is asked. It was with considerable sadness that I recently heard that the delicious lobster omelette we used to buy in El Rosario for 75 cents was now going for three dollars.

I HAVEN'T BEEN EVERYWHERE in Baja; that's one of the reasons the peninsula keeps calling me back. I've lost count now of the off-pavement journeys I've made in Baja but there's always a new place to go or an old favorite to be revisited.

My most faithful source of as-yet-unvisited places is Gerhard and Gulick's *Lower California Guidebook*. A few hours with G&G and I can always find someplace I want to go whether it's for a weekend or a week. As I said earlier, Gerhard and Gulick is well out of date so far as the main road goes, but for the sideroads, those trails that lead to the best places in Baja, *Lower California Guidebook* is still the best source of information. So stick with good old G&G, make allowances for the changes that have taken place since the last revision and they won't lead you astray. And of course their notes on historical points of interest as well as the flora and fauna are impeccable.

To give you an idea about off-pavement excursions in Baja, let's pick a couple or three interesting-sounding places and see how we go about getting there. We'll choose one that's not too far south, a place you can go for a long weekend. For the other two, let's go on down the main road south of Ensenada and take a couple side roads that might be incorporated into a longer trip.

For the short trip, we'll go to El Alamo, an old gold-mining town where there were once around 5000 people, which is now nearly deserted. For the longer trips, we'll visit El Marmol, a once-booming onyx town that Joseph Wood Krutch wrote about in *Forgotten Peninsula*, and San Borja, the northernmost of the great stone churches. After that I'll tell you about some of the other places I've been that make good off-pavement excursions.

EL ALAMO

While El Alamo is not known as one of the glamour spots of Baja, it nevertheless has its points as a place to visit. First of all, the road to El Alamo from Tecate is an excellent introduction to the kind of off-pavement motoring you should plan to do a lot of in Baja. Second, the route not only takes you through a variety of different kinds of country but also through some of the prettiest mountain scenery on the peninsula. Third, there are enough side roads, off-shoots, backtracks and confusing trails to offer a bit of a challenge to your navigational ability. And finally, it's within an easy long weekend's drive from the Los Angeles area.

The easiest way to get on the trail to El Alamo is to cross the border at Tecate. A tourist permit isn't required in this area, so there's no need to hesitate at the border. There's a Tepeyac insurance office on the right just past the Mexican border station where that formality can be taken care of and the highway that runs between Mexicali and Tijuana is at the bottom of the hill at the traffic signal. There's a liquor store on the right that's convenient and after making the turn to the left (east) at the signal there's a bakery (*panaderia*) on the left hand side a couple blocks farther along.

Following the auto club map and Gerhard and Gulick, drive east out of Tecate on the paved road toward Mexicali. This is 2-lane blacktop and while there's almost always a slow truck or bus to be followed, the country is rolling and pleasant.

The turn-off we're looking for is just over 16 miles east of Tecate and it's easy to keep track of where you are by checking off the little settlements as you pass through. About a mile before the turn-off there's a gas station, *Servicio Delgado*, which is marked on the auto club map. This is a good place for a final fill-up with gas as there's no dependable source of gasoline between the turn-off and El Alamo.

Unlike most of the side roads encountered in the lesser populated areas of Baja, the turn-off we're looking for is almost impossible to miss since there are several hand-painted signs with names of ranches on them. Some of these refer to ranches that are on our route. "Jacomun," for instance, and "Rancho Neji." So here we leave the pavement.

After stopping to lock the hubs and relieve some of the pressure in the tires, we head south. The road is graded for the first few miles and there are fences along here as well. Later on we'll get away from fences and that improves the scenery.

Keeping track of your progress is reasonably simple. Here's the system we use when we're heading off on a new road for the first time. When leaving the pavement, we write down the mileage shown on the odometer, then add the appropriate number of miles to the next point shown in Gerhard and Gulick. In this instance it is 2.9 miles and here the road turns right while the road straight ahead leads to Jacomun, a cattle ranch. As the odometer comes up on the calculated mileage, we watch for the turn and when we find it, we get set for the next point. This is another ranch, Las Juntas, cattle ranch across a meadow on the right and it's 1.1 miles. Next comes Rancho

Neji, 5.4 miles, and here, for the first time since leaving the highway, you know exactly where you are because there are several signs proclaiming that this is in fact Rancho Neji.

You're not likely to get seriously lost in Baja as long as you're paying attention and provided you don't panic if the expected sideroad or ranch isn't precisely where you expect it to be. Baja has changed considerably since the book was written, so one ranch may not be there at all and there may be two others instead. And the side road you're looking for may have disappeared completely. Or perhaps you just didn't see it. Try not to worry. Press on in what seems the logical direction, aiming for the next point. When you arrive at an unmistakable landmark you'll be able to re-orient yourself. If you are genuinely lost and on the wrong road, keeping track of the checkpoints makes it a lot easier to get back to where you aren't lost anymore.

It doesn't do to fret overmuch about taking a wrong turn in Baja. I used to be embarrassed when I took a wrong turn and had to turn around in some rancher's front yard but I got over that. It's all part of the Baja game. Provided you know how to get back, of course.

Actually, the road through this area is not difficult to follow. It has had sufficient traffic over it to be plainly discerned almost everywhere.

After passing El Compadre, which is about 18 miles from the pavement, the road climbs over a pass into another valley and here you begin to see pine trees. It is sensationally beautiful from here on, one of the most beautiful mountain areas in Baja, with big granite boulders, lots of trees, lovely meadows and miles and miles of clear, fresh air.

If you want to do a little side road exploring along the way, read ahead in your Gerhard and Gulick for a place that sounds interesting. Along this route, for instance, there's an abandoned tungsten mine near Rosa de Castilla. This mine, called El Fenomeno, was a very large producer during World War II and reportedly furnished over two percent of the world's tungsten supply at that time. The maps show it to be off to the right of the road and the only way to find it is to keep trying various tracks that head off in the right direction. We did this recently and while the first trail looked promising, it ended where a large oak tree had fallen across the road in a lovely shady glen. We had to back and fill to get turned around, then returned to the main road and tried the next set of tracks.

This trail led back into a canyon with big trees, green grass, wildflowers, plenty of firewood and everything that would be required to make an ideal place to camp. The canyon became narrower as we continued and after a mile or so we came to a small stream. The trail turned up this side canyon, running alongside the stream and though the road was in poor condition we crept through without difficulty. After fording the stream we climbed the bank on the other side and here, we deduced, was where the shops for the mine had been located. There were a couple foundations where buildings had once stood, a few old tires, a broken flywheel, and under a huge tree there was a work table made of planks that were black with soaked-in oil. On the table there were still various bits of machinery such as part of a roller bearing, a large bolt, half a metal hinge and several unidentifiable scraps of metal. Nearby were a couple small holes that appeared to have been dug rather recently but as these obviously could not have supplied two percent of the world's tungsten we knew the mine had to be farther ahead.

The trail continued over a sharp rise, then skirted the shoulder of another canyon. Here the grass had grown up, leaving only a hint that there had been a road here at one time. We followed this for perhaps another half mile and the road dropped to the bottom of a narrow, twisting canyon where the bushes scraped against the sides of the car. It was getting dark by this time, the sun having already disappeared behind the hills, and when we came to an open knoll where it was possible to turn around we decided we'd better find a place to camp before it was pitch dark.

But we're supposed to be going to El Alamo, not El Fenomeno, and that's on down the road.

Continuing south past the Indian village of La Huerta, you meet a well-traveled east-west road that has come down the east side of the mountains and is on its way to Ojos Negros and Ensenada. Our route jogs left (west) here, then south again, climbs over a rise and then coasts down a long slope toward the Ensenada-San Felipe highway.

This point on the highway is about 55 miles south of the Tecate-Mexicali highway and about 38 miles east of Ensenada. But after the drive down through the Sierras, it's easy to imagine that you're a lot farther than that from civilization.

To get to El Alamo, go east (left) on the highway for 12-13 miles, then turn south again. Up until now there have been few navigational problems as there have been a minimum number of side roads on which to get confused. But after leaving the highway there is an area that is criss-crossed with all manner of tracks and trails, making it much easier to wind up going in the wrong direction. A compass in your car is extremely helpful in such areas as this since what you have to do is keep working your way in the right general direction every chance you get and be prepared to backtrack when you make a wrong turn.

I couldn't for the life of me give you explicit directions for getting to El Alamo. The best I can tell you is that it's roughly south-southwest of the place where you leave the highway. G&G says its 11.3 miles by one route and 13.0 miles by another so I'd say if you have gone much more than 15 miles without getting there that you'd better shift your search to the north and west because you're probably on a dead end road heading toward Rancho El Florida or La Poza. But don't feel bad if you are, I've been there too.

But El Alamo, once you get there, is well worth the trouble. Gold was discovered in the area in 1889 and according to Gerhard and Gulick there were as many as 5000 people in this vicinity at one time. Other sources give considerably smaller numbers for the maximum population of El Alamo but it was undoubtedly a sizable place once, judging by the number of foundations for buildings that have now disappeared and the quantity of tailings there are piled up around the mines. There are some old gold mill buildings on the edge of town but these date from a later period, probably World War II or later. The last mining was done here in the mid-1950s and when we were last at El Alamo there were only seven families still living in the town. There's a small, unused church with a cast concrete tower, the shell of a municipal office building with a fading "1948" on the facade, a small store, a local mechanic who dispenses gasoline from a drum and not much else besides a landing strip that doesn't appear to do much business either.

I like such places as El Alamo. I enjoy poking around the old buildings, examining the abandoned machinery, looking at the few houses that remain, imagining it the way it was when the boom was at its height—or how it would be to live here today. Luckily, there are many such places in Baja.

When it's time to head back for the border, there are several alternatives to choose from. Back on the Ensenada-San Felipe highway you could go to either of those places and have paved road all the way home. Or you could go on east beyond Valle de Trinidad on the pavement, then go south across the dry lake and stay off the pavement the rest of the way to San Felipe. Or you could work your way back north and take the road past Laguna Hanson and rejoin the Tecate-Mexicali road at El Condor or La Rumarosa. I'd suggest the route past Laguna Hanson for this trip since it involves a minimum amount of pavement.

A short trip such as this gives you a good feel for finding your way in Baja. The country is beautiful, there are fascinating places to visit, there's a minimum of traffic and while it's something of a challenge it's still not so uninhabited as to cause any serious difficulty even if you do get lost. If you're going to be spending any time off the pavement in Baja, such a trip as this is an excellent introduction.

Typical "good" road in the hilly central part of the peninsula.

GETTING TO EL MARMOL

El Marmol, you'll recall, is an abandoned onyx mining town roughly 65-70 miles east and slightly south of El Rosario. Getting there, once you leave the pavement, presents a slightly different kind of challenge than the El Alamo trip.

Okay, south we go and while you're on the pavement you don't need anything except the auto club map to keep track of where you are, although Gerhard and Gulick is handy for the history and points of interest. Stop at Tijunana for car insurance, Ensenada for last minute supplies, Maneadero for tourist permits, then on to the south.

The highway is 2-lane blacktop all the way to Cabo San Lucas but don't plan on making the kind of speed you do on a typical U.S. highway. There are not only lots of sights worth looking at but the road isn't engineered for turnpike speeds. Some of the bridges are narrow, there are likely to be occasional road crews and the sharp turn ahead may or may not be marked with a *"Peligro"* (danger) sign. The first hundred miles or so south of Ensenada is through agricultural country and Baja farmers, like farmers everywhere, don't always look both ways before pulling onto the highway where they putter along at a very modest pace and then turn off again, all without any kind of signal. So drive with a certain amount of restraint.

There's an additional bit of caution required once you get onto the newer pavement south of Camalu since much of it is quite narrow (only 6.5 meters as compared to 7.5 meters, the standard width), with no shoulders and occasional abutments that encroach on the paving.

After you leave the agricultural area, which ends about 130 miles south of Ensenada, you travel across flat, level country for a while, then climb up into the hills before coming down into El Rosario. Gasoline, beer and basic grocery supplies are available here in case there's anything you need.

The highway turns left (east), follows the wash through town, then heads south. If you're feeling adventurous at this point, seek out the unpaved road that continues on up Rosario wash beyond the local landmark, El Castillo, a rock formation on the north side of the wash that resembles a castle. This route is a bit sandy for the first few miles but presents no problem for 4-wheel-drive vehicles and is far more scenic than the highway. The road stays on the right hand (south) side of the arroyo and it is here that you will see your first giant cardon and your first boojum trees. It is worth stopping to introduce yourself and make their acquaintance.

The road then climbs out of the arroyo, goes over what we call the Dreaded Red Hill, a long steep grade that overlooks the arroyo, and into some even prettier boojum country. Keep heading west, more or less, don't take any side trails that will return you to the arroyo and you'll come to an old copper mining area called Sauzalito. The road is wider here for a few miles, having been scraped out to fit the big trucks that were used to haul sand and gravel from a nearby wash up to the new highway during its construction. When you come to the abandoned mine buildings stay to the left and you'll go through even more boojum forests before rejoining the main road just west of Rancho Arenoso.

If you stay on the pavement after leaving El Rosario, you will see that it by-passes most of the old landmark ranches that we used to count on as navigational aids, although you still get a glimpse of the old road from time to time.

When you get in the vicinity of San Agustin (55-60 miles from El Rosario or about 30 miles east of Arenoso), take the side road off to the left that leads to the ranch. When you get to the ranch, look toward the east for dim tracks that go off across the plain. There are several sets of confusing tracks in the first mile or two. These ultimately lead back to the highway but what you want to do is continue in a direction that is just slightly north of east.

At several places along this old road there are deep-sunk ruts that were originally made by the heavily laden onyx trucks on their way down to the Pacific coast. At other times there are newer tracks that parallel the deeply worn road. When you come to a windmill on the right, El Marmol is not far away.

If you're fascinated by ghost towns, and who isn't, you'll like El Marmol. Located on the edge of what Gerhard and Gulick accurately describe as a "bleak plain," here are the remains of a town where several hundred people once lived.

The onyx quarry is over a small rise to the right as you come into town and there you can pick up chunks and chips of high grade onyx. There is some abandoned machinery standing around and it's easy to visualize it the way it was when the huge blocks were lifted out of the quarry, then swung around on the long boom to be stacked awaiting shipment.

Onyx was first quarried at El Marmol around 1900 and the American company that developed the property imported Indians from the mainland to work there. The demand for onyx dropped off after the development of ornamental plastics and in 1958 the quarries were closed for the last time. For a few years the owners kept caretakers there in case the world got tired of plastic desk sets but that hasn't happened and El Marmol has been totally abandoned now for several years.

The schoolhouse, which is probably the only one in the world that is made of solid onyx, is the sturdiest building left in town and will no doubt be standing when the last traces of the other buildings have disappeared. The house of Senor Brown, who was the manager of the mine, is across a wash on the side of town opposite the quarry. It was quite a nice place, and up until 1971 we used to have picnic lunches on his porch, looking out over the town. Then they built the new house at San Agustin and the doors, frames, windows and whatever else was usable were ripped out of Senor Brown's house and it too is now settling toward collapse.

The old motor pool and garage still stand, however, and around at the back there are still several big iron truck wheels with solid rubber tires. It's easy to imagine how those rode over the trail down to San Agustin and then to the shipping point at Puerto Santa Catarina.

When you've had your fill of exploring El Marmol you can return to the highway by the road you came in on or you can go on to the south. If you choose the southern route, you drive past the quarries, then cast around for the track that will take you up over the hill and on south. You can see this road from the town but finding the right track may take a little time. This road, though somewhat washed out in places and pretty slow going, is easily followed and readily negotiable in a 4wd vehicle. The best part of this road is that the other end brings you out on the highway near La Virgen, another spectacularly beautiful area of huge granite boulders and tall boojum trees. It makes a wonderful place to camp provided you take a sideroad far enough off the highway that you can find something to burn in your campfire.

This little sidetrip to El Marmol is also good experience for the off-pavement Baja traveler. It goes to a place that is genuinely remote and where you're very likely to be completely alone. In half a dozen or so visits to El Marmol, we've never been there when there was anyone else in town and it is eerie to realize that only a few years ago this was a busy little company town complete with hard-working

Northernmost of the Jesuit churches is this one at San Borja.

miners, devout housewives and enough children to require a school.

I can't guarantee it will be deserted when you make your visit, though. The way things are being built in Baja these days, I wouldn't be surprised to encounter a billboard at San Agustin reading, "El Marmol Hilton, 10 Miles."

Honestly, though, it doesn't seem likely.

TO SAN BORJA

If you've done any reading about Baja California, you're no doubt aware that Catholic missionaries established a chain of missions that encompass the entire length of the peninsula. You may also know that the most impressive of these were built by the Jesuits and that the last of their great stone missions was built before Junipero Serra started his trek to the north to establish the more famous chain of missions in our own state of California.

The first mission in Baja was founded at Loreto in 1697, then the missionaries moved both north and south to do their work and save the heathen natives from their sinful ways. There are several of the great stone churches still standing and all are worth a visit. Luckily, most of the best missions are well off the beaten path and this makes them even more interesting, to my way of thinking.

San Borja was the last mission to be built by the Jesuits before their expulsion from the New World in 1768. The Dominicans took over then and replaced the original adobe church with the stone building you can see today. The assortment of diseases brought by the white man almost literally wiped out the native population and the

End of the pilgrimage; the tip of the peninsula at Cabo San Lucas.

last resident priest departed in 1818. Since then it has had almost no formal maintenance, yet there it still stands, a monument to missionary zeal. A building such as San Borja would be impressive wherever it was encountered, but there, absolutely in the middle of one of the greatest nowheres in the world, its presence is absolutely staggering.

All right, then, let's go to San Borja. You'll find it on the map by following the highway south of the junction of the roads from Ensenada and San Felipe, then taking the branch road that goes left (east) toward Bahia de Los Angeles. This junction is clearly marked on the new highway. Follow the road toward L.A. Bay for about 30 miles, then turn right (west) for an additional 22-23 miles to the mission.

The road to Los Angeles Bay is a "good" dirt road, well traveled and easily followed. It goes past a deserted gold mining area, Desengano, after about 8 miles and this is a good place for a picnic. There is lots of beautiful country through here with an abundance of really choice elephant trees and in the spring there are usually lots of wildflowers.

After about 27 miles there's a large dry lake off to the left and you know at this point that the turn-off to San Borja is only 2-3 miles ahead. The road toward San Borja goes up a wide canyon and it's fairly easy to make a wrong choice of roads as you make your way toward the mission. No serious matter, though, as the sideroad will either peter out or take you to a rancho and when this happens you simply go back to the fork and try the other branch.

As your odometer tells you you've traveled 20 miles since turning off the road to L.A. Bay, keep watch for a high, dark bluff on the left (south). The mission sits at the bottom of this bluff in a little valley. You round a bend and are surprised to find yourself there. If you're not knocked out at seeing this huge stone structure in such a remote location, you're a lot more difficult to impress than I.

The front of the mission looks up the valley and the chapel is always open. The altar is extremely simple, there are no benches and the late afternoon sun shining through the windows make fascinating patterns on the walls. There is no priest at San Borja but a local fiesta is held there on October 10th each year and residents for miles around come to celebrate with their friends and neighbors.

Some of the shells collected during a morning on Conception Bay.

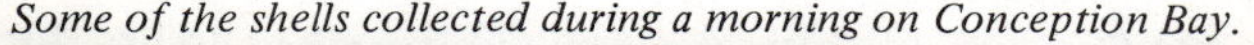

To return to the highway, you continue to the west. The through road turns right just as you get to the mission and if you were busy looking as you drove up, you may have missed it. This road is fairly slow and rough but it's no worse than the road you were on earlier; it rejoins the paved road at Rosarito after about 30 miles.

PICK YOUR OWN

After you've gotten the feel of off-pavement travel in Baja, you can begin to search your map and your Gerhard and Gulick for new places to go. Certain places will catch your fancy and tease your imagination, or at least they do mine. A trip I looked forward to for a long time, for instance, was down the west coast from Punta Canoas. We finally made it last spring and though it wasn't quite as remote as I had expected (we saw three other cars), there wasn't a permanent dwelling between Santa Catarina and Punta Rosalillita, which was delightful. It was cold and windy, though, which spoiled some of the fun though it would be a fine place in summer when you could enjoy the surf and the lovely, deserted beaches.

But there are so many good places to go. The stone churches, for instance. Don't miss any of them that you can possibly get to, and there's some kind of road to all of them. Santa Gertrudis is about 25 miles from El Arco and well worth the trouble. San Javier is the best preserved of all the original churches and it's an easy 20-25 miles inland from Loreto, or you can drive almost 50 miles up Arroyo San Javier from the old main road just south of Santo Domingo. Mission San Luis Gonzaga is also a delight. It's about 22 miles from the paved road south of Villa Constitucion at a little oasis that's just what you need after the drive.

I'd also recommend visiting the Comondus deep in their own canyon. And La Purisima as well. And Calamajue Wash. And Los Angeles Bay. And Las Flores. And Pozo Aleman. And Cadeje. And most anyplace.

However, I wouldn't really suggest the west coast below Villa Constitucion. I've never driven there but I've flown down that coast, and while there are dunes out there that don't have a tire track on them, the coast north of Miller's Landing is much prettier, as well as being closer to the U.S.

And when you finally make that trip to the tip of the peninsula, if you're saddened by the number of fancy resorts, seek out the unpaved road that runs counterclockwise around the tip from San Jose del Cabo. It goes past many nice, quiet beaches before getting back to civilization again.

The peninsula is full of wonderful places to visit. You could make a career of it. I wish I had the time.

YOU MAY ALREADY be an experienced camper and know everything you want to take on a trip to Baja. But at the risk of omitting something that should be included, I'm going to throw in this chapter with the basic information about what to take along.

The first essential, so far as I'm concerned, is a checklist. Maybe you're better at organizing than I am and won't need one but inevitably, no matter how often we go camping, we forget something if we don't use ours. We start with our basic list while we're still in the planning stages, add to it as we think of special things, and when the time comes to pack up, we're usually pretty sure to have all the essentials.

To make this list as practical as possible, I'm going to list the things we carried on a recent trip down the west coast to Guerrero Negro.

First came the camping gear:

Cots	Sleeping bags
Tent and poles	Coleman lanterns
Blankets	Laundry bag
2 small tarps	Folding chairs
Camp stove	Folding table
Folding stand for stove	2 ice chests
Folding toilet	Small funnel
4 gals white gas	Leather work gloves
Small axe	Shovel

Then the emergency stuff for the car. This included my "Peace of Mind Kit" plus:

2 jacks	Tool box
2 sand mats	Big hammer
Lug wrench	Hacksaw blade
Tire pump	2 spare tires

We also carry two compartmented tucker boxes into which go our general cooking utensils plus some supplies:

12-in teflon skillet	Cooking utensils
1-qt saucepan	Can opener
2-qt saucepan	Bottle opener

4-qt stewpot
Coffee pot
Plastic glasses
Aluminum foil
Wax paper
Eating utensils
Napkins
Paper towels
Corkscrew
Cereal bowls
Sugar
Salt
Pepper
Dishpan
Paper plates
Coffee cups

In cardboard cartons we had 12 gallons of water in 1-gallon plastic bottles, three boxes of food, an empty box for coats and sweaters, plus our "convenience" box that contains such things as insect repellant, extra mantles for the lanterns, extra flashlight batteries and bulbs and other miscellaneous extras.

That left those things that go in the front of the car in the side pockets, glovebox, under the seat and in various cubbies:

Attache case (maps, guidebooks, notebooks, etc.)
Binoculars
Pocket compass
2 flashlights
Dustcloth and wiping rags
Pliers
Tire gauge
Screwdriver
Large knife
Litter bag (and extras)
Sunglasses
Extra prescription glasses
20 4-ft lengths heavy cord
Kleenex
Small crescent wrench

Also in the front goes our first aid kit:

Snake bite kit
Boric acid
Salt tablets
Ace elastic bandage
Cough drops
Bandaids
Laxative
Kaopectate
Diarrhea pills (prescription)
Pain pills (prescription)
Aspirin
Halazone tablets
Extra chapstick
Burn ointment
Suntan lotion
Antiseptic salve
1-in. surgical tape
Gauze
Cotton
Tweezers
Small scissors

And finally there was the food we took along. Because the food you take on any camping trip is so much a matter of personal taste, I'm going to hedge at this point and rather than list everything we carried, I think it might be more helpful to talk in general terms about what we have learned about eating along the trail in Baja. Let's take it meal by meal.

First, breakfast. Because we camp in a tent and have an hour or an hour-and-a half's steady wall-to-wall work in breaking camp and repacking the car, we like to have a quick breakfast when we're on the

Compartmented boxes like this are convenient when camping.

move. This usually means a small can of fruit juice, instant oatmeal or dry cereal, coffee and let's go.

For those lazy days when we aren't moving our camp, we think a more leisurely breakfast is called for and we like to have canned ham (or bacon) with eggs (fresh if possible, dried if not) or with hotcakes. A favorite hotcake with us is Flapstax, which requires only the addition of water, not milk, as does that old stand-by, Bisquick. We also like what we call fried bread, which can be an English muffin, a Mexican roll or a slice of real bread tossed into a hot pan with a lump of butter and allowed to sizzle to a crusty brown. We're also far enough away from the true old campfire campers that we find instant coffee palatable for breakfast as well as all other times when we're camping.

Then comes lunch. Without doubt, lunches are the most difficult meals to plan. You seem to have more of them to fix, for one thing, since a visit to a resort or motel will generally cover dinner and breakfast but you'll be back on the road again by the time lunch rolls around. At home we're mainly sandwich eaters for lunch but once the bread isn't fresh any more, sandwiches lose most of their appeal. So what we've finally settled down to is an assortment of snacks that can be eaten with crackers and beer. We like salami and cheese and can eat that fairly regularly, chicken spread and deviled ham go down all right occasionally but aren't what I'd like for a steady diet, Spam will do once in a while, as will sardines, canned tuna and other such things that can be finished up in one sitting. We never fire up the stove at lunch time because of the time it takes away from the more interesting things we might be doing, so if it's cool and we think we're going to want coffee with lunch, we fill a Thermos at breakfast time for that purpose. But we admit we've never really solved the lunch problem—except that we don't waste much time over it.

And dinner. When you've been traveling all day, have found a good camping place, unloaded half the stuff out of the car, pitched the tent, put up the cots, unrolled the sleeping bags, gathered stones for a fire ring, dragged in wood for the evening fire, filled and pumped up the stove, serviced the lanterns, put the cooler on its stand, lined up the tucker boxes and finally the time has come to sit down and enjoy the sunset, you've earned a decent meal. So for dinners—and the pre-dinner cocktail hour we always enjoy—we try to do something a little bit special. Because water is more important than weight in Baja, we've done no more than make an occasional experiment with the lightweight freeze-dried foods that are so much in favor by those who have to carry everything on their backs. Some of these are very tasty but all take a quantity of water, as well as being considerably more expensive than conventionally packed foods. So we go for the more exotic things that come in cans or boxes. And it's surprising the variety of good things that come in cans these days, especially the meats that don't have to be refrigerated—good ham, roast beef, even turkey and gravy. Because it greatly simplifies the cook's work—as well as being handier to eat around the campfire—we prefer meals that are mostly one-dish main courses. But that doesn't mean you have to have beef stew or chili and beans every night. Some of the menus we enjoyed on a recent trip included chicken cacciatore with rice, green beans and a tossed green salad (all prepared at home and eaten the second night on the trail), a pseudo-Mexican dish called Tamale Joe which consists of a can of tamales with a can of chili and beans mixed in, covered with sliced cheddar cheese that is allowed to melt and then sprinkled with crumpled up corn chips. And one night at Scammon's Lagoon we had a canned pork chow mein dinner that was complete not only with Chinese noodles but was topped off with fortune cookies (one of which said we should prepare to take a long trip).

In general, we have found that canned foods tend to be a bit bland for our tastes and for that reason we carry such things as seasoned salt, garlic salt and onion flakes to zing up the flavors. We usually treat ourselves to a couple fancy desserts from the gourmet section of the local department store and have had babas au rhum, brandy cakes and peaches in wine on occasion. Most of the time we settle for canned fruit for dessert, or boxed cookies.

If you miss your salads once you're away from the supermarket, there are some substitutes that may satisfy you. Cucumbers will last as long as you have ice and when sliced are crisp and refreshing with a bit of salt or a drop or two of salad dressing. Marinated mushrooms, artichoke hearts, celery hearts and asparagus plus salad dressing make a nice substitute for a green salad, as do those things that go under the name of canned relishes.

Between-meal snacks and cocktail-hour snacks can also tax the ingenuity as we seem to get away with more of those when we're camping than we do at home. We like dry-roasted peanuts as a cocktail snack, as well as cheese and crackers, but the seasoned crackers that are fine in small quantities tend to become overpowering unless taken a few at a time. For on-the-trail snacks, I like those little boxes of raisins and usually try to keep a box or two handy in the glove box.

It is typical, I think, that we always take far more than we eat on such a trip but that's obviously better than doing it the other way and having to be sparing with food toward the end of the trip for fear of running out.

In addition to our planned menus, we also fill one box with what we call our emergency food supply. We don't plan this down to the last meal-by-meal menu but we do try to make sure we have at least enough calories to see us through a week's short rations in case we ever really need it. We never have yet but I'm always glad to have it aboard.

As with all other equipment you use on a trip to Baja, the amount of space you have for carrying things largely dictates your approach. If you have lots of space, as in a station wagon-sized Jeep Wagoneer or an International Travelall or a pickup camper, you can let yourself go and not worry too much about the bulk of the food you're carrying. If you're traveling light in a dune buggy, however, where every cubic inch of space is critical, you may very well want to go after the condensed or dehydrated variety and depend on local water supplies rather than having the liquid pre-packed into the containers.

There are also small ranches at several places along the way where a traveler can get a meal. We have patronized these very little, generally preferring our own company at meal time, but it does sometimes make a pleasant break from doing it yourself.

In any case, whether you fix all your own meals or whether you eat somebody else's cooking every chance you get, there's no real reason to bore yourself to death with unimaginative victuals.

THE ART OF PACKING

As I consider myself something of an expert in this line, I'd like to offer a few hints about the art of efficient packing. There are two things that are most important; first, having everything in a proper container that can possibly go into a proper container and, second, having some idea which container it's in.

Proper container, to me, means a sturdy rectangular box and I regard the 10-by-12-by-17-in. beer carton as ideal. These are strong, stack well, aren't so big that you can't lift them when full and have good, reasonably dust-free lids. They are convenient to load, have fingergrips for lifting and because the three dimensions are all slightly different you can, by turning one this way, one that and putting another on end, fill up almost any rectangular space and make up a nice tight load.

For a medium-sized vehicle, so far as I'm concerned, a car-top carrier is pretty nearly essential for efficient packing. Up on top go all the basic camping gear and this is an ideal out-of-the-way place for it as it seems like everything that goes inside a tent is odd-shaped or shapeless. These things, when carried down below, utterly destroy any otherwise sensible packing plan. If you're on a go-one-place-and-stay vacation to the mountains, you may be able to stand having everything jammed into the back any old way; but on a move-every-day tour of Baja, it can drive you straight out of your mind.

Putting the camping gear on top leaves the back of the vehicle relatively clear and uncluttered for everything else. It is first of all fundamental that the heaviest things should go as low in the load as possible and as far forward as possible. This keeps the center of gravity lower and results in a far more stable vehicle when the going is rough. Not everything can go low and forward, of course, so you have to temper the placement of your containers by deciding what you're going to have to get at during the day and try to locate those things at lunch. And the folding chairs to sit in at lunch time. And the table. And the tucker box with the eating utensils. And the folding toilet.

To take care of all those odd-shaped things that don't fit into cartons and don't find a home anyplace else, I made a simple rack that fits up next to the roof of my Bronco. There, cinched down with bungee cord, rides the axe, shovel, camera tripod, stove stand, bucksaw, tire pump and a short-handled rake I find extremely handy when clearing a campsite of cactus balls, small stones, or cow patties. I also built long shelves that go along each side over the fender wells, making a flat place to stack things on and creating handy little cubbies underneath that are just right for 1-gal. cans of Coleman fuel, gloves, siphon, funnel and other small objects.

When you're on any sort of serious trip in Baja, you'll be carrying enough things that no load is going to have everything just where you want it, but by using easy-to-handle rectangular containers, whether you obtain them at the liquor store or make them yourself—and they're marked on both ends as well as the top so you can tell what's in them—the whole thing is greatly simplified.

Camping
is What You Make it

NO DOUBT ABOUT it, camping is what you make it. And, like the food you take along, the camping equipment you find most satisfactory depends to a large extent on how much room you have to carry it. If you're cramped for space, as in a dune buggy or a CJ-5 Jeep, you gravitate toward the lightest, most compact gear you can find. For a tent—if you want a tent at all—you might consider one of the Thermos Pop Tents. A Pop Tent goes up fast, with small fiberglass rods that give it an igloo shape when it is erected. It has a sealed-in floor, insect-proof openings and with it you can relax and not have to worry about nocturnal visits from the crawly things. In a Pop Tent you will probably do without cots, which are always bulky, and instead use one of the inflatable air mattresses that fold down to cigar-box size. And for sleeping gear, down-filled mummy-type sleeping bags are not only light in weight but will squeeze down to almost nothing in bulk. The temperatures in Baja are very mild, even in winter, and it's very unlikely to be even as cold as freezing—so you don't need arctic-weight gear by any means. For extra warmth when needed, we always take thermal underwear along as it adds heat without bulk and can give just the right amount of insulation when sitting around the fire in the cool of the evening.

To fit into minimum space, there are comfortable, lightweight folding chairs. Or if even those are too bulky, a simple, metal-framed canvas stool is more comfortable than sitting on the ground.

There is also a variety of lightweight cooking equipment to be considered: a 1-burner Coleman stove, for example, or one of the famous folding Primus stoves that burns denatured alcohol. Both of these are quite efficient and keep the amount of fuel you have to carry down to a minimum. A nesting set of cooking pots occupies as little space as possible, yet lets you survive in a civilized manner.

For a minimum-bulk load, efficient packing is a must and to me this means fitted containers where everything has its exact place, fits snugly and without any wasted space. Again, rectangular shapes fit together with less wasted space than round ones and while they haven't yet put beer in square cans, it's surprising how many things

A camp along the old road near beach south of San Jose del Cabo.

you can find that do come in rectangular packages when you begin to seek them out.

The larger camping supply stores that specialize in back-packing equipment (see "Sources") can be especially helpful both for lightweight equipment and for efficiently packaged freeze-dried foods. There are a number of meal-in-a-box dehydrated meals to be had and these include such things as beef stroganoff, roast turkey with dressing and, yes, even a pretty palatable hamburger. Because lightweight items are highly specialized, and this is true of the food as well as the equipment, they are also more expensive. So if space isn't critical, you can save money by buying the more conventional varieties.

When we had our Bronco we used a car-top carrier for all our overnight camping equipment and that worked fine. Now that we have a Jeep Wagoneer, we don't use a carrier but get all the stuff in the back end after removing the back seat. Either way, it is possible to carry enough gear to camp in pretty near home-style comfort. It's probably true, however, that Parkinson's First Law also applies here and that no matter what size vehicle you have, you'll take along enough stuff to fill it up.

A tent is not often a necessity in Baja, so far as the weather is concerned. We have done without one many nights in Baja and, in fact, really prefer to set up our cots under the stars when the weather is mild and the wind isn't blowing a gale. To an urban dweller like me, there's no thrill that quite compares with lying on my back and looking at the sky, trying not to let my eyes close until I've seen a shooting star.

When sleeping outside, though, I'm also enough of an urban dweller that I'm not comfortable sleeping on the ground. Not only because the contours of the ground never seem to fit me but I don't like the idea of sharing my bedding with whatever happens to crawl by. On a folding cot I feel completely relaxed and with a medium-weight sleeping bag, a blanket and a light tarpaulin to keep the dew off, I've been cozy on even the coolest Baja nights.

We do take a tent with us to Baja, though, and it goes up whenever the weather is cold, which it certainly can be at times, or when the wind is howling, which it sometimes does. When the climate has really gone sour, either with cold or wind, we set up the tent, use it as a kitchen first, then turn it into the bedroom when it is time to retire.

You don't need a heavy sleeping bag in Baja's mild climate and a 3-lb bag filled with Dacron 88 is adequate as well as being reasonably priced. My wife's is a 5-lb model, one of the multi-layered types where you can select one, two or three thicknesses over you, but it is heavier than is needed except in very rare cold weather.

For cooking gear, a 3-burner Coleman stove adds a welcome touch of luxury as it doesn't occupy all that much more space and makes it possible to keep more things going at the same time. There are also 2-burner models, of course, and some of these are extremely compact and efficient to permit the luxury of 2-burner cookery without unnecessary weight or bulk.

The problem of illuminating what's necessary around camp is not an easy one. The Coleman-type gasoline lantern that you pump up probably offers the best light for its size but there's something about the hiss of a gasoline lantern that seems inappropriate in the wilds. But I confess I haven't found anything else that will replace it. A further disadvantage is that you always have to carry a supply of spare mantles. I took six extra mantles on our recent trip to La Paz, used them all and had to borrow one from a friend to see us through. The bottled-gas variation on the pump-up theme has some advantages but the extra cylinders are awkward to store and while you can find white gas along the way, you're unlikely to encounter any bottled gas.

Windbreak at rear made this camp at Scammon's Lagoon a cozy one.

There are large battery-powered electric lanterns—with some models that also plug into the cigar lighter outlet in your car—but these are even heavier and bulkier than a gasoline lantern as well as being more expensive.

Chairs, stools and tables come under the heading of necessities for comfortable camping, as far as I'm concerned. We use inexpensive aluminum-and-plastic folding chairs from the cut-rate drug store and these, plus a 24-by-24-in. table I made with a square of half-inch plywood and the brackets and legs from a TV tray table, serve us very well.

On an extended trip, we take two ice chests, one large and the other larger. By filling one of these with solid chunks of ice (the larger one will take three 25-lb blocks) and leaving it closed until all the ice has melted in the other, we can have ice for a week or more. If the melted water is drained off as it accumulates, the ice will last that much longer and adding slabs of dry ice will even further delay the melting process. Ice chests should be pretty rugged for travel in Baja and those molded styrofoam coolers don't stand up to the rigors of Baja travel very well.

Ice is sometimes available at several places in Baja but we have found these sources to be rather undependable. We got ice cubes from Senor Diaz at Los Angeles Bay on one trip, for instance, but found that he had none at all available on our next visit.

We try to practice a reasonable amount of water discipline in Baja, wasting just as little as possible, draining our ice chests into our plastic water bottles (and marking them "wash") and making every cup go just as far as we can. In normal traveling in Baja, we have found that we use about one gallon of water per person per day.

There are thousands of beautiful campsites in Baja for you to choose from so I'll just offer one of my famous handy hints. When it is windy, we move the car up at right angles to the tent and then put up one or two small 5-by-7-ft lightweight canvas tarpaulins as a windbreak. We have a couple extra tent poles to use with these and then anchor them to an ice chest or spare tire to keep them in place.

One of the camping aids I worked out for myself is the 20 lengths of heavy cord I am never without when going camping. Cut in 4-ft lengths, these are handy for a myriad of duties—tying down a windbreak, putting up a clothesline, bundling up a sleeping bag, serving as a shoe lace or for dragging wood into camp. Knotted on each end they will not unravel and I'm seldom without one or two in a hip pocket from the time I cross the border until I'm home again.

Since we started this section by extolling the virtues of a checklist, I think it only appropriate to end it with a few words about a trip log. This is also an essential part of the Baja traveler's equipment, to my way of thinking. My wife keeps ours and at any odd moment of the day, you may see her working on her notes. It is useful for many purposes, not only as a precious souvenir of this trip but also extremely helpful when you get ready to plan your next trip and can't remember how long it takes to get from El Rosario to Arenoso via the Dreaded Red Hill. We also use it for making notes about the things we should have brought but didn't (and would inevitably forget if we didn't write them down) and when we're off in country we don't know, we make a detailed mile-by-mile log noting the mileage when we left the main road, where we took that fork, how far it was to the dry wash where we almost got stuck and what time it was when we first began to realize we were lost. In such instances as these, the log becomes invaluable since it makes it far easier to retrace our steps to get back to some point where we aren't lost anymore. And this, on occasion, can be important to your health as well as to your peace of mind.

One of the author's special favorites, the handsome elephant tree.

BAJA IS A place where there is lots of interesting vegetation to look at. Strange things, too, for Baja has more unusual plants than any place I know.

Technically, the greater part of the peninsula is Sonoran desert though the southern area south of La Paz begins to get into the tropical zone. In the northwest corner of Baja, the flora is much like that of southern California, but once you approach El Rosario, the true Sonoran desert plant life takes over and then extends, with variations for altitude, moisture and latitude, the rest of the way south of La Paz. Many of the plants in Baja will be familiar to those who are acquainted with the desert in southern Arizona and southeastern California. But it's also different in Baja, many of the familiar plants having evolved in a slightly different way than their relatives in the north or on the mainland of Mexico. You'll find ocotillo in Baja, for instance, but though it is readily recognizable as the same plant common north of the border, the individual stalks that are straight, whip-like and almost delicate in the north grow crooked and present a much more rugged and bush-like appearance. The two plants have different botanical names to distinguish between them, the straight-limbed variety being called *Fouquieria splendens* and the Baja type *Fouquieria peninsularis.*

There are also many of those extra-special plants that are peculiar to Baja and which, most unmistakably, say "Baja" to anyone who has seen them there. The first of these is the boojum tree or, to give it its proper Mexican name, the *cirio*—or its proper botanical name, *Idria columnaris*—also called the candle tree because it is tall and slim and its blossoms occur in a "flame" at the tip. These are found in great numbers between El Rosario and El Arco and come in all manners of weird and wonderful shapes and sizes.

After the rainy season, the short, straight, twig-like branches put out small, bright, green leaves, these turning yellow and dropping off in drier times and the stems rolling in on themselves to form thorns. The main trunk of the *cirio* varies from green to yellow to brown and

Girl meets Boojum. The author's wife pats a friend on the head.

at the driest times of the year, the small branches appear almost black. In some areas near the coast where the air contains more moisture, a parasitic moss will be seen hanging from the branches to give them a somewhat decadent appearance.

Boojum trees are often amusing in the shapes they take. The ordinary ones are tall, slim, straight and graceful, coming to a single point at the top. Others divide near the top into two or three smaller trunks, sometimes reaching up, sometimes winding about like the arms of a Balinese dancer. Still others do even stranger things—like bending over to the ground to form an arch and then springing up again. Where two are growing close together, their limbs sometimes intertwine; our favorite camping place near La Virgen is marked by such an affectionate pair that we call them "The Lovers."

Another characteristic of boojum trees is that almost all of those growing together in a grove will be about the same height. Near the abandoned copper mine at Sauzalito, for instance, there are groves of very tall ones and here you only occasionally see a smaller one. In another area only a few miles away on the slope south of El Arenoso, there are stands of boojums only half as tall.

If you become enamored of the boojum tree, as I am, you may be glad to know that some of the larger commercial cactus gardens (see "Sources") have them for sale and that they will survive in the southern California and Arizona climate. My personal boojum isn't the healthiest specimen I've ever seen but a friend who lives in Santa Barbara has one that seems to thrive on life in a redwood tub.

When you look at a boojum tree you can be assured that you are looking at a genuine curiosity of the plant world. It is the only species of that genus and its nearest relative, which isn't very near at all, is the ocotillo. All the boojum trees in the world (not counting those transplanted out of their native habitat) grow within a radius of 125 miles and they grow naturally no place else than in Baja except for a few across the Gulf of California on mainland Mexico. So a boojum is something special in many ways.

Incidentally, the "boojum" after which the *cirio* got its nickname first appeared in Lewis Carroll's poem, "Hunting of the Snark," in this paragraph:

" 'But oh, beamish nephew, beware of the day,
If your Snark be a Boojum! For then
You will softly and suddenly vanish away,
And never be met with again!' "

To which I can only add, I can think of worse ways to go.

Second ranking as a curious plant that is at home in Baja and only rarely found elsewhere is the elephant tree. This plant, known to the Mexicans as *copalquin*, has a grayish white trunk and limbs and these are fat and stubby, thus accounting for the familiar name. The

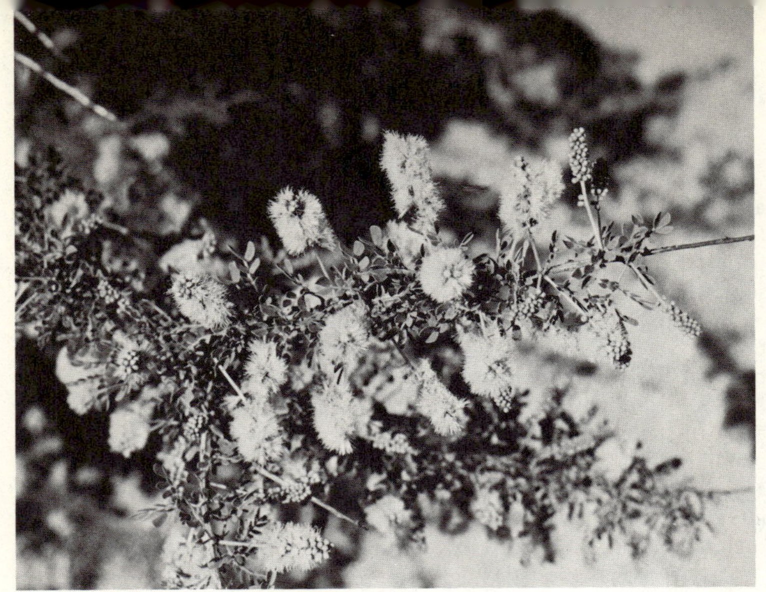

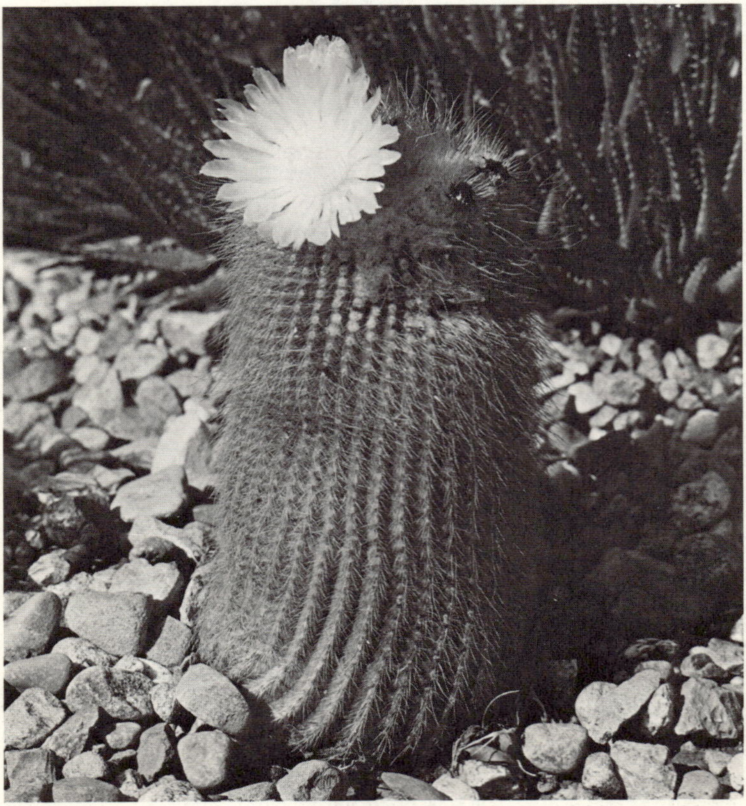

CAM WARREN PHOTOS

Blossoms like these are found in profusion in late spring.

Above, the needle-like spines of the cholla. Below, a nice senita.

Left, the century plant is worth seeing even after blossoms have dried .and blown away. Right, yucca blooms lead to yucca pods.

Cholla is deceptive; soft to look at but hard to get out of the hide.

elephant tree is common south of San Agustin on the main road and south of San Luis Gonzaga on the bay. Like the *cirio*, to which it is not related, the *copalquin* has small, bright, green leaves after the rains and these turn bright yellow during the drier seasons. Elephant tree wood, though soft and porous, makes a good campfire but, like most desert fuel, it does burn rather quickly. The elephant tree puts forth pinkish blossoms at infrequent, irregular intervals as it, like the boojum, only blooms after the right combination of moisture and heat has taken place.

In southern Baja there is another elephant tree, the *torote*, but although there is a family resemblance, it grows lower to the ground, is slimmer, does not have so white a bark and lacks the character and chubby charm of the *copalquin*.

Also typical of Baja is the *cardon* or giant cactus. The Great Cactus at the top of Aguajito grade is a *cardon* and the hero of *Journey of the Flame* regarded the *cardon* as his symbol of Baja and, according to the book, "died alone in 1902 at the Great Cardon, near Rosario, Mexico, with his face turned toward the south." It may not be exactly the same Great Cactus as ours, but I like to think it is.

There are also two other variations of the *cardon* found further south in Baja, the *cardon pelon* which has no thorns (and is gnawed upon by cattle in dry times) and *cardon barbon*, which has abundant spines growing on the ridges like a narrow hair brush. These last two do not have the size, dignity, or charm of the Great Cactus of the north. The *cardon* blooms in late spring—we have seen a sprinkling of their flowers as early as mid-April—and these appear near the top of the trunk. The blossoms are large, creamy cones which, like other

This curious succulent was found blooming in early summer in Baja.

cactus flowers, are incongruously delicate on such a rugged plant.

The fourth plant I associate with Baja and nowhere else is the *palo blanco* tree. The white bark of the *palo blanco* is as striking as the lovely green *palo verde* familiar to us in the southwestern U.S. It is found in sandy washes in the southern half of the peninsula and is a slender, graceful, lightly leaved tree that puts out small, lacey, yellow blossoms in the spring. Like the *palo verde*, the *palo blanco* is also related to the acacia and has the same type of leaves and blossoms.

If you are any kind of a desert buff, there are dozens, maybe hundreds, of plants that will seem familiar to you when you see them in Baja. There is a large variety of cholla in Baja, for instance, everything from the charming silver cholla, so called because of its soft, gray appearance, to the less attractive chain fruit, buckhorn and club varieties. Cholla blossoms are something special in any desert as they are exquisitely beautiful and range in color from bright yellow to paper brown. The petals of the cholla blossom are waxy and it is almost certain that if you look into the cup of half a dozen you will find at least one in which a bee is disporting himself, rolling about in the deep pollen and giving every indication of having a wonderful time.

One of the most famous of the cactus in Baja (though it is also

Candelilla's rich, white sap was formerly used for making candles.

found elsewhere on the mainland and in southern Arizona) is the *pitahaya*, which is known to us as organ pipe cactus. It was the pitahaya harvest that was the signal for the native indian of the peninsula to begin his annual good times complete with eating the sweet red fruit until his stomach stretched as tightly as a drum and participating in what the missionaries regarded as unspeakable orgies and unmentionable promiscuity with all the members of the opposite sex that happened to be in the neighborhood at the time. And if another tribe happened to be nearby, perhaps they'd even wander over there and have a little inter-tribal orgy as well. The time of the pitahaya was about the only season that the native tribes could find enough to eat during the year, so perhaps a little overindulgence is understandable. If you happen to be there when the pitahaya is ripe, you should try it but be careful not to eat yourself into an orgy as it is likely to upset your civilized digestive system.

There's also *pitahaya agria*, or sour *pitahaya*, and this is even more common along the peninsula. This is a common, sprawling, dark cactus with arms about three inches in diameter. The sour pitahaya fruit is tart to the tongue and quite refreshing in small quantities.

Candelilla is another common plant in the northern part of the peninsula. The stalks are about the diameter of a thick pencil, grow

Even in summer you can find interesting dried plants in Baja.

three to four feet tall and when one is snapped off, a thick white sap oozes from the break. It is said that the sap was formerly collected and boiled down to make candles. I've never seen a candelilla candle but it sounds like a reasonable story.

There is a very wide variety of cactus in Baja, as you would expect. There are many *bisaga*, or barrel cactus, in a variety of sizes, and these put out a crown of bright yellow blossoms in late spring. And many varieties of the paddle-shaped beavertail and pricklypear and these mostly show pink to red blossoms in the spring. All cactus bear fruit and that of the pricklypear, called *tunas*, is a bright red berry shape and also moderately palatable. Down beside bigger cactus plants, or in among the rocks, you will also find little pincushion cactuses and collections of larger and smaller fuzz balls known as hens and chickens.

Cactus blossoms begin to appear in mid and late spring but the best displays are found in early summer. As a general rule, the smaller the plant, the earlier it will bloom, the tiniest ones coming on at the time of the spring wildflowers, the larger ones making their appearance later. We have seen some of the smallest varieties blooming as early as the first part of February—the tiny fuzz balls that hide in the lee of a protective rock and put on a pale yellow flower no bigger than half an inch across. Cardon blossoms can come as early as mid-April but don't get to their peak until May.

The many members of the yucca and agave families found in Baja also bloom in the spring and, in their own way, are as spectacular as the cactus when it is in flower. The yucca blooms are common in April and their blossoms are a rich, thickly packed cluster of ivory-colored blossoms that form in clumps larger than a football. The agaves put up tall, slim stalks to show their flowers—some as tall as 25 or 30 ft. When these are first springing up—and some grow so quickly that you can almost see them get taller—they resemble nothing quite as much as a giant stalk of green asparagus. Then the flaps open on the stalk and serve out handsful and armloads of yellow blossoms. The Parry agave, from which is made *pulque* and tequila, are especially spectacular in this respect, with profusions of bright flowers.

Even if you are not there at the moment when the yuccas and agaves are at their peak, you can also enjoy them later. The blossoms of the yucca become a lovely, creamy beige before turning brown and if there is no serious wind, these will stay intact for a considerable length of time. When the fruits are thoroughly dried, the winds carry away the seeds and their pods, leaving a single knobby twig. The dried agave stalk will stand for months, first drying and turning brown and then continue to lend a dignified enchantment as they stand silhouetted against the sky.

As Professor Krutch points out in *Forgotten Peninsula,* many of the plants with which you may be familiar in California and Arizona are somehow bigger, brighter and more spectacular in Baja. And as you go further south, approaching the tropic zone, what may have been a rather insignificant little vine in the northern climate becomes wildly luxuriant in the south. He gives as an example the *tecoma* which, at his home in Tucson, was a small bush with orange-red flowers but in southern Baja grows to the size of a small tree, as much as ten feet high, and puts out a mass of yellow blossoms.

The spring wildflowers are a special thing all their own in Baja. Perhaps it is because there is so little civilization to interrupt them but we have witnessed displays there that outshone anything we have ever seen north of the border. We have encountered tremendous expanses of sand verbena, for instance, and on one trip to Los Angeles Bay we passed through an area where, mixed in with yucca and elephant trees, the ground was covered with their lovely pink blossoms as far as you could see in any direction.

Not every year is a great year for wildflowers in Baja, their appearance depending on just the right combination of moisture and warmth coming in the proper proportions and at the most propitious intervals. We were lucky enough to be there on an extraordinary spring a few years ago, however, and in four other spring visits have never again seen so many in so many places. There are always at least some wildflowers to be found in the spring, however, and Baja has never let us down in this respect. Many of them will be familiar to you, of course, as they are mainly similar to those in southern California and Arizona—desert mallow, phacelia, sacred datura, penstemon, desert zinnia, brittlebush, crownbeard, coreopsis, goldfields and so on.

All the plants in Baja should be left where they are, of course, as a special permit is required to bring them across the border into the U.S. If a particular one takes your fancy, you can probably find it at one of the larger cactus gardens and there I have found my own boojum, a small *cardon, senita* and a *pitahaya*. If my *pitahaya* ever attains full growth and has a crop of bright red fruit, you're all invited over for the orgy.

A favorite Boojum tree along the road south of Calamajue wash.

With so many roads to choose from, plan on getting lost sometimes.

Careful is
What to be in Baja

CAREFUL is what it's most wise to be when you travel off the pavement in Baja and I'm going to wind up this handbook with some words of caution that you'll do well to heed. Because Baja is so unfettered by regulations of the type that surround us no matter where we go in the U.S., there is a temptation to let down the restraints once you get beyond the international border. You may get away with being careless in Baja but it is wise to remember that you can't call a cop if you happen to get in trouble, that the automobile club won't come and get you if your car breaks down, that you can't phone for an ambulance if you get hurt and that you're more on your own and more dependent on your own resources than you're likely to be anywhere else you travel.

It is, first of all, much safer to travel in company with at least one other vehicle, especially off the pavement. In this way you can support each other. You can tow each other out when you get stuck, you have more heads to put together when an important decision must be reached and if one of the vehicles is disabled you have the security of knowing that somebody can go for help and that you're not going to be there for the rest of your life.

That isn't to say that you don't dare leave the paved road by yourself. We do it with a certain amount of impunity but not if we're going to be any serious distance off the main highway. There's certainly an abundance of traffic on the pavement these days and if you're not so far away that you can't hike over to the main road for help, you should be all right. But if you're going someplace that's really remote, such as the west coast between Punta Canoas and Miller's Landing, and your wheels stop turning, you could be in serious trouble. That's the least-visited, least-populated part of the peninsula and you could spend days or weeks on some of those roads over there without having a single vehicle go past. There are no supplies there, neither gasoline nor food, and you'd be foolhardy to visit that part of the peninsula if you were by yourself.

Before you leave home, give your itinerary to a friend and tell this friend when you expect to be heard from again. Then, if you are

If you do break down, a friendly local dog may come to help you.

utterly lost, your car immobilized with a fractured crankshaft and you are suffering from a broken leg you got by falling off a cliff, there's a chance you can be rescued before it's too late. Travelers have perished in Baja, as you've no doubt read in the papers, and while it isn't as common as it once was, it can still happen.

If you're lost, and somebody knows you're lost, your chances of being found are very good these days, thanks to the increasing number of Baja buffs who know the peninsula as well as you know your own back yard. And with the number of skilled pilots who regularly fly over Baja, you can almost certainly be located if you stay with your vehicle, put out distress signals and do whatever else you can to attract attention.

If this ever happens to you, the best thing to do is make yourself as comfortable as possible, set up your emergency program regarding food and water, and waste just as little strength as possible. Try to find an open space where you can put out an SOS signal—either strips of light-colored clothing held down with rocks, or with stones, or light-colored sand, or anything else you can find that will contrast with the ground you put it on. An SOS sign doesn't have to be huge; good contrast is more important.

Also be ready to make a signal when the rescue planes come looking for you. For this it is important not to run yourself completely out of gasoline when you're lost. That last gallon in your tank is far more important for use in making signals than it is to take you another few miles. A raw gasoline fire makes a healthy black smoke that can be seen for miles and if you mix engine oil with it, the smoke will be even more dense. As a signal fire, put about a quart of oil in a skillet and keep it ready. Then, when the sound of an airplane engine is heard, put about a pint of gasoline on top of it and toss in a match.

When you succeed in attracting the plane's attention, show signs of life by waving something—a white undershirt, for instance, or a white sheet, if you happen to have one along. If the pilot sees you he will circle to get a better look and will probably waggle his wings to tell you he sees you. Sooner or later he will fly away, leaving you to wonder if he will see to it that a rescue party is dispatched, but you can be fairly confident if he has circled you since Baja pilots can usually recognize signs of distress.

Unless you know exactly where you are, where help can be reached and are sure you have the strength and the supplies to get there, it is always better to stay with your vehicle. This is extremely important. It isn't easy to wait to be rescued but trying to walk out is just about the most foolish thing you can do in any serious emergency. That takes reserves of strength you're not likely to have and generally

Which way should we go? Three heads are often better than one.

assures that you'll be in that much worse shape before you're found.

A vehicle, because it has a regular shape and is fairly large, is far easier to spot from the air than an individual on the ground by himself. You perhaps remember reading about a young student pilot who crashed near El Rosario a few years ago. Though his plane was soon sighted and reached by rescue parties on the ground, he perished because he did not stay with the aircraft but tried to walk to the coast.

In an emergency, be lazy. Use as little energy as possible. Don't try to clear a landing strip the first day you're there. Do what you can to make your situation known—an SOS sign, a signal fire ready, light-colored cloth to wave—but don't exhaust yourself. If you have to stay there a few days you'll have plenty of opportunity to expand your signalling facilities with bigger SOS signs, stacks of brush you gather for your signal fires and big arrows on high points aiming at your camp.

Plan your food rations and try to arrange them so you won't have all the dry things to eat at the end. Food isn't terribly important in an emergency where you have shelter and don't waste your strength. It probably wouldn't hurt you at all to fast for three or four days and it wouldn't kill you to go without food for a solid week. Water is important and about three days is all you can last without it. Of course you shouldn't waste water but neither should you try to do without it as that will simply bring on heat exhaustion. If your water supply is short, try to stretch it out with those things in your food supply that are water-packed—stewed tomatoes, for instance, or peas, or green beans. Avoid physical exertion as much as possible, especially during the heat of the day, and if it's hot, take salt tablets from your first aid kit.

If your vehicle is stuck in a canyon where it is likely to be hard to see from the air, move your rescue station out into the open where it can be seen more readily. Even toilet paper, held down with small stones, can make a good SOS sign.

Incidentally, if you do ever require a formal rescue operation in Baja, you should offer to reimburse your searchers for their trouble. There isn't a volunteer rescue organization that picks up the tab for such things and it's surprising how few people who are saved through some volunteer's efforts offer even as much as a thank you.

There are other emergencies with which you may be faced in Baja. Your car can break down, even on the main road, and while this isn't likely to be a disaster, it is inconvenient. But you can easily hitch a ride to the nearest point of civilization and either get help or secure the necessary parts to repair your machine. If you suffer such a breakdown, it is wise to have your car towed to the nearest ranch so you can leave it there rather than out in the wilds where it might be looted or stripped. The local residents are very compassionate people and will look after your wife if you must leave her there for a few days while you go back to Ensenada or San Diego for a new axle or transmission.

Injuries which require medical attention beyond the scope of your first aid kit can be serious in Baja as emergency medical facilities are few and far between. If a member of your party is seriously injured or ill, the best plan is to head for the nearest ranch or settlement that has a working air strip. It would be of little help to camp out on one of the deserted strips since many of these are not really usable except as a possible landing place for a plane that is in serious trouble and few pilots will take a chance on crashing just to see if they can help. Some of the larger ranches, such as Santa Inez, and even the fly-in resorts, have 2-way radios and can get a plane in to evacuate an injured person even though it won't happen with as much dispatch as you feel is necessary.

Because medical help isn't readily available in Baja, you should, for your own safety, be extra wary when you are doing anything that might lead to an injury. If you're changing a tire, block the wheels so the car can't roll off the jack. When you're chopping wood, practice good woodsmanship and don't split your foot along with the kindling. If you're climbing in rocks, don't risk a bone-breaking fall and be careful where you put your hands lest you disturb a dozing rattler.

As long as you and Baja are fairly new to each other, you'll probably be respectfully cautious. It's when you begin to take Baja for granted that you're likely to get careless. I know. It has happened to me. Down near Santa Inez, watching the Mexican 1000 race, I lost my balance and fell off a rock and broke a collarbone. At that time the nearest pavement was about 150 miles away and believe me it was no fun riding over those roads with the ragged ends of the bone grinding together. And only last winter my wife and I took off for what we expected to be a pleasant weekend between Ensenada and San Felipe and got caught in a rainstorm. Overconfident fool that I was, I not only hadn't put in a shovel, a big jack, or the chains, I hadn't even taken the tent. As a result we spent one whole day stuck in the mud near El Rodeo, slept in the cab of the pickup that night and finally got out on Monday. That wasn't a disaster, either, but we could have been a lot more comfortable sitting out the storm in a tent. So don't get overconfident either.

Something like the sea, Baja can be fickle and capricious. She has her moods and it's always best to be prepared when she decides to play one of her tricks on you.

FINALLY, just one last word. Baja isn't the place it once was. There was a time when any traveler was welcome wherever he went in Baja. The pavement has opened the floodgates and personally I can't blame some of the local residents for regarding Americans as an evil that has to be tolerated for the money they spend rather than as friendly visitors. The Baja residents who don't live along the highway aren't over-exposed to Americans and you'll find them a relatively unsophisticated people, gentle, kind, hard working and a little shy. They won't cheat you, they won't steal from you and they aren't going to take advantage of you. This off-pavement part of Baja is a wonderful place, one of the last good places left on this earth of ours. So do all you can to keep it that way, won't you?

Sources for Baja Things

THE FOLLOWING IS a list of sources where specialized (and sometimes hard-to-find) items likely to be of interest to the Baja traveler may be found. The list doesn't cover every possible source, obviously, but I hope it will offer a hint for those who need it. The subjects are organized in the order in which they appear in the text.

BOOKS AND MAPS

Any good bookstore will be happy to order books they don't happen to have in stock. A few that carry off-pavement and books about Baja in stock are:

Automobile Club of Southern California, 2601 S. Figueroa, Los Angeles, Calif. Baja map and guidebooks.

Dick Cepek (see entry under Tires and Automotive)

Dawson's Book Shop, 535 N. Larchmont, Los Angeles, Calif. 90004. Has largest selection of books about Baja. Also publishes Baja California Travel Series.

Desert Magazine Book Shop, Palm Desert, Calif. 92260. Free catalog.

TIRES AND AUTOMOTIVE

Dick Cepek, 9201 California Ave., South Gate, Calif. 90280. Specialist in wheels and tires for off-pavement vehicles. Also has good selection of what he calls "Baja Proven" auto accessories and camping gear. Good rack of current Baja publications including guidebooks, McMahan Baja map, *4wd Handbook,* etc. Dick is also an excellent source for advice about off-pavement vehicles and Baja. Free catalog.

Sidles Custom Shades, Box 3537, Temple, Texas 76501. See-through shades to keep the sun out. Free catalog.

J. C. Whitney, 1917-1919 Archer Ave., Chicago, Ill. 60616. Old-line mail order source for automotive stuff (such as defroster fans) you may not be able to find anyplace else. Free catalog.

CAMPING EQUIPMENT

Local sporting goods stores and the larger department stores—such as Sears—carry a pretty complete line of conventional camping gear. But if it's specialized equipment you're looking for, you might try the following:

Eddie Bauer, 417 E. Pine St., Seattle, Wash. 98122. Free catalog.

L. L. Bean, Inc., Freeport, Maine 04032. Free catalog.

Famous Department Store, 530 S. Main, Los Angeles, Calif. 90013. Free catalog.

Herter's, Inc., Waseca, Minn. 56093. Free catalog.

Kelty's, 1801 Victory Blvd., Glendale, Calif. 91201. Free catalog.

ABOUT THE AUTHOR

The author of *Baja Handbook* James T. Crow, lives in Costa Mesa, Calif., and works for Bond/Parkhurst Publications when he can't find an excuse for going to Baja. His travels in Baja have been extensive and he has made more than fifty trips below the border gathering information and impressions about the peninsula.

A journalist, he was the editor of *Road & Track* magazine from 1966 to 1972 and is now publisher of *Pickup, Van & 4WD*, a new magazine from Bond/Parkhurst devoted to light trucks. His other books include *Four Wheel Drive Handbook* and *Survival of a Species: Elephant Seal.*

Editor: Ed Reading
Designer: Hal Crippen
Art assistant: Sonja Keith

Photos not otherwise credited were taken by the author